D1083904

Elizabeth, The Winter Queen

*In precious memory of my Grandfather, Elliot Gorst, Q.C.
Poet, farmer, linguist, and generous friend and inspiration
to many people*

Elizabeth
The Winter Queen
Jessica Gorst-Williams

Abelard . London

ISBN 0 200 72472 X

Abelard-Schuman Limited
A Member of the Blackie Group
450 Edgware Road
London W2

Printed in Great Britain by Robert MacLehose and Co. Ltd.
Printers to the University of Glasgow

CONTENTS

ILLUSTRATIONS

ACKNOWLEDGEMENTS

I am very grateful to Mr. John Raymond for suggesting the subject to me; to Mary-Geraldine O'Donnell for her help and for the enthusiasm she has shown throughout the writing of the book; to Elspeth Rhys-Williams and Alexander Bathory for their interest; and, above all, I should like to thank my husband for his optimism and encouragement.

CHAPTER ONE

Elizabeth, Princess of Scotland, daughter of James VI and Anne of Denmark, was born on 19 August 1596, at 2 o'clock in the morning. There was a discreet pause while her father waited to see if this child would survive the rigours of 16th century obstetrics and the harsh climate of Scotland. He did not have to wait long to discover that the child had inherited her mother's robust constitution and was unlikely to succumb to any of the hazards around her. King James then began to worry about the expense of the christening.

This was his second child, his first daughter. There could be no ceremony on the lavish scale of two years before when the Chapel Royal had been rebuilt to accomodate the guests for the christening of his first child, Prince Henry. He thought of ways to economise and he decided to delay the ceremony until the winter had set in and few guests would be able to make the journey to Holyrood House. When he was told that, despite this precaution, a large attendance was expected, he stipulated that the guests must bring their own food.

He then turned his mind to the problem of a name. There was no difficulty about that. The child would have to be called Elizabeth after the Queen of England. King James looked across to the rugged hills of his country and sighed. He despised Scotland. The older he became the more resolutely he determined to get away from it. Here he was trying to control the turbulent nobility and fanatical clergy of a country so poor that it could not raise enough money even to pay his servants or to cover the cost of his food bills. There was only one solution and that was for him to secure the throne of

England. That, King James had convinced himself, was the proverbial land of milk and honey.

He was, after all, the immediate heir to the English throne after Queen Elizabeth's death. His great-grandmother had been Margaret Tudor, Henry VIII's elder sister. Even now he corresponded regularly with the Queen's foremost minister, Robert Cecil. But there were complications: Queen Elizabeth herself had seen to that. She might be past love and child-bearing, but she was not past mischievousness and deviousness. She read the underlying concern in King James' too persistant enquiries after her health and she determined to keep him on tenterhooks.

"Regard her well," she had said once, provokingly pointing to James's cousin, Arabella Stuart, another possible claimant to the throne, "for she is not as simple as you may think. One day, she will be even as I am, and will be lady-mistress." And here she underlined one of James's problems. Although he was closest in direct line, he was a Scot and born in Scotland. There were those who said that no alien such as he could lawfully inherit the crown of England. No such barrier existed for English-born Arabella and there were powerful men in England who would rather pull the strings for a puppet-queen than have a king to rule them.

And then there were those who cited Henry VIII's will. In it he had laid down that the succession should pass to his children Edward, Mary and Elizabeth and then, if they died childless, to the children of his younger sister Mary, wife of Charles Brandon, Duke of Suffolk. Their elder daughter, Frances Brandon, had married Henry Grey and borne him three daughters. The eldest was the unfortunate Lady Jane Grey and Queen Elizabeth had taken good care that the other girls did not marry. But despite her vigilance, Edward Seymour, Earl of Hertford, son of the Protector Duke of Somerset had managed secretly to wed Lady Catherine Grey. Two sons were born to them: one survived. But Queen Elizabeth had always maintained that the marriage was invalid, so Edward, Lord Beauchamp's claims were weaker than they appeared.

Fortunately for James, Arabella's supporters were Robert

Cecil's enemies and Cecil was making sure that the crown should come to James. With Queen Elizabeth's other ministers he was constantly asking her to name James her heir. For the sake of peace, they told her. But there was time enough, she always said, and continued to deny the facts to herself. Long ago she had banned mirrors in her palaces so that she could not see the lines which she suspected furrowed her forehead and the pallor that disfigured her cheeks. King James remembered all these things as he looked towards the hills; moving his hand to his dagger at the smallest sound; thinking of the robust child who had brought such things to his mind.

There was nothing to do but to continue to flatter his ageing kinsman. He did not like flattering other people, he much preferred being flattered himself. But it had to be done. He would invite Queen Elizabeth to be sole godmother to his daughter. A letter must be written. Although she had already "graciously" agreed to be the only godmother to his son Henry, would she, the formal parchment asked, now "accept [the] dedication of this princess"?

When she received the letter, Queen Elizabeth saw through it all, as she usually did, and took two months to reply. Eventually she wrote rather offhandedly to the English ambassador in Scotland, saying that "although we did scarce believe at the first but having so lately christened his son", she would accept Elizabeth as her god-child. She then amused herself by deliberately delaying any mention of a christening present for the young princess until after the christening, in order to embarrass King James.

King James, however, was too busy to be upset. Having dedicated his daughter entirely to Her Majesty in England, he had now set about wondering who was to look after the child. That in itself was a difficult decision. James remembered the humiliations of his own childhood. The governor of a royal child held a powerful political weapon in his hands. He must choose someone whose loyalty to him was beyond question. Lord Livingstone seemed to fit the bill. His loyalty was known and his father had proved as true to James's unfortunate mother, Mary Queen of Scots. So, although objections were raised that Lady Livingstone was a "notorious Papist", in the end King James decided on Livingstone and arranged for Elizabeth to go to him at Linlithgow Palace, one of the loveliest places in Scotland.

King James had given Linlithgow to his wife just after their marriage. His grandmother, Mary of Guise, although she had thought that "Scotland was a poor country, destitute and void of all good commodities that used to be in other countries", had confessed that she had "never seen a more princely palace" than Linlithgow. It lay in the heart of Scotland between the Forth and the Clyde, splendidly conspicuous among the unenclosed fields and the farmers' cottages made of turf and wood. The Stuart succession had been formally acknowledged there in 1371; the Court had resided there before the battle of Flodden; and Mary, Queen of Scots, the child's grandmother, had been born there.

The Livingstones did their job well and, within three years, another child, Margaret, was put into their care and joined the nursery at Linlithgow. Elizabeth who, throughout her life, found babies rather distasteful, did not pay any particular attention to this younger sister. Her affection already rested elsewhere.

She loved her brother, Henry. Every word he spoke she hung onto with as much tenacity as she clung, in a less abstract sense, to Lady Livingstone's skirts when something frightened her. In fact Henry was very seldom at Linlithgow, but that tended to increase her devotion to him.

He was growing up at Stirling and already he was fluent in several languages; rode well; sang; danced; shot at archery and pored over the works of Terence, Cicero, and Phaedrus. Elizabeth had not learnt these facts from Henry, who hardly spoke to her when they were together. Nearly everything she knew about him she had learnt from the servants at Linlithgow. How often she had sat in the dark near the kitchen hoping to hear news of Henry, but sometimes, accidentally, hearing more disquieting news.

It was through that medium that Elizabeth became aware that the sweeping hills and fragrant heathers of Scotland and the pervasive calm of Linlithgow belied the insecurity within the realm.

Her father seemed to be constantly in fear of his life. When he

4

came to see Elizabeth and jovially put his arms around her, she could feel under his clothes the mail shirt which she guessed he wore for protection. Then there were times when the King and his Court were expected at Linlithgow and never arrived. Even more confusing there was talk that Queen Anne was intriguing to take her two daughters away to Dunfermline Castle against their father's wishes. In the event none of the prophesied upheavals took place. King James survived, and Queen Anne's vitality was destroyed in the grief at the death, first of her son Robert, who hardly survived his baptism, and then of Margaret. Constantly pregnant and constantly miscarrying, Queen Anne was for the time being too tired to destroy the peaceful uneventfulness of Linlithgow. It was up to other forces to do that.

Late on the night of 27 March 1603, there was a loud knock on the gate of Holyrood House. This was followed by so much commotion inside the Palace that King James, clad in his night-shirt and night-cap came into the anteroom to find out what it was all about. By the time he was ready, an exhausted traveller had gained entrance and was demanding to see the King. He introduced himself as Sir Robert Carey, and King James, stepping forward with as much dignity as he could muster under the circumstances, begged to know what business could have brought him here at such an hour of the night. In fact he knew perfectly well what Sir Robert had come about, but it seemed better to dissemble. Sir Robert was a courtier. Unless he stood well with the new king he knew that all his lucrative appointments could vanish overnight. A week before he had sent a confidential messenger to tell James that Elizabeth was mortally ill. The doctors had given her only another three days to live, he had said. Now, as bearer of the welcome news of her death, he knew those appointments were safe. He might even hope for better things as a reward. So, when the Council had tried to stop him, he had escaped and ridden at breakneck speed. His bruised face bore witness to the fact that it had not been an easy journey.

When he saw the King, he knelt before him and "saluted him", in his own words, "by his title of England, Scotland, France and

Ireland". The King gave him his hand to kiss and welcomed him. He asked politely how the Queen had died and then he asked if there were letters from the Council. Sir Robert replied that there were no letters, but there was a "blue ring" which would prove to his Majesty that what he spoke was true. King James took the ring with a solemn gesture, which belied the sense of triumph that he felt. Three days before it had been slipped from the finger of his great rival in England, he was being told. He rubbed his own fingers over it. So even the longest-lived were mortal in the end, thought the scholar-king for just a flicker of a moment. Then, ordering the messenger to have a good night's sleep, King James turned on his heels and retired to bed.

He woke in the morning to put into action the prearranged plan which enabled him to leave Scotland within ten days. He had given strict instructions about who was to come with him and who was to stay behind, and those who should stay behind included his wife and children. He had dutifully kissed Queen Anne in front of a large gathering of spectators and then he had addressed his subjects in Scotland, settling, as he put it rather complacently, "both Kirk and Kingdom". There was no time for him to say goodbye to his children; not even the youngest one, Charles, who was considered too frail to make the journey to England. King James had begun to feel uneasy about those other possible claimants in England. News had already reached him that people were stocking up grain in London in fear of civil war and he had not heard, because news travelled so slowly and unreliably, that the Council had quelled their fears and the price of grain was back at its normal level.

And so he set off on 5 April 1603. With him came an immense retinue of Scots and when he crossed the border he was met by members of the nobility of England. People thronged the streets to greet him. In one place he fired a canon, in another shot a deer, and in yet another he authoratively ordered the execution of a thief (an order, incidentally, which was not carried out). It was all like a dream come true. What did it matter that no-one seemed to understand his Scots accent. There were other ways of indicating his goodwill. He began to hand out knighthoods much more

1. King James I, Anne of Denmark and their Family. Elizabeth stands on her father's left, clasping Frederick's hand. Their children are in front of them.

2. The Castle and Town of Heidelberg, painted by Jacques Foucquières about 1618.

liberally than he paid compliments and, by the time he reached the outskirts of London, he felt so confident of his inheritance that he lingered, expressing his delight in everything he saw, cunningly masking his reluctance to attend Queen Elizabeth's funeral. He had always had a dread of funerals and even now, in his moment of glory, it assailed him.

Robert Cecil, who had made a thorough study of King James' character, in the same way that he had studied his predecessor, knew this. He made it clear that it would be unnecessary for anyone to tell King James that a severe outbreak of the plague was pervading Stepney and gradually encroaching on the environs of Whitehall. It would be extremely inconvenient if the new King did not come to London soon and seal his inheritance. For, despite his immediate proclamation and Cecil's assurances that there were no supporters for the other claimants, there were people who objected to the Scottish King. And so nothing was mentioned of death and disease and very little was even spoken about Queen Elizabeth, whose spirit nevertheless seemed to permeate London. King James would have been foolish if he had imagined that it could be eradicated so quickly. The verve she had instilled into England, the memory of forty-four years during which she had led England to greatness was not so ephemeral that it could be destroyed by the uncouth figure who had taken her place. The stresses to which he had been subjected as a child left James finding it difficult to maintain his balance when he walked and impossible to talk without his tongue lolling out of his mouth. He could never compete with his predecessor.

The English public, as always, tolerated his physical disabilities and pretended not to notice them. However, James judged correctly that a certain aura of romance was needed and that it would be difficult for him to provide that. Queen Anne could perhaps fulfill that need. He began to make arrangements for her to come to England, but it was not until June that the new Queen set off on her journey south.

There had been various reasons for delay. Anne would not travel if Henry did not come with her, but when she had gone to collect him from Stirling Castle, his guardians, the Earl of Mar himself was in London, had refused to let him go without the King's permission. This had induced the birth of another still-born child. King James had then agreed that Henry should travel with her, but this had been followed by a message saying that her Danish ladies, who had been with her for thirteen years, must be replaced by English noblewomen. Queen Anne threatened and sulked, but nothing came of it. It was easy for James to be firm when he was safely in England. The Danish women must go, and then he added insult to injury by dispatching some of Queen Elizabeth's dresses, altered to fit Queen Anne, rather than allowing her to have new clothes made.

It was some time before Queen Anne recovered from her various shocks and tantrums and was able to go with Henry to Linlithgow to collect Elizabeth. When they arrived it was to find that Elizabeth had a fever and was suffering from a severe nose-bleed and a temperature. She could not bear, she had announced before becoming ill, to leave Lady Livingstone. No-one could or would make her go.

The illness only lasted long enough to delay her journey for a few days. Then it was decided that she must travel at a different pace from her mother and brother, stopping more frequently and missing the more amusing entertainments.

Elizabeth was too homesick to mind that. A new guardian, Lady Kildare, had been found for her. Elizabeth, wearing a dress which was much too hot for midsummer, sat dully at her side, watching the horses straining to drag the heavy coaches over the primitive roads; politely accepting the presents which were offered to her and noticing perhaps, something of the subtle change from the poverty of Scotland to the nascent wealth of England.

For most of the time it was a miserable journey. Lady Kildare's husband, Lord Cobhan, had been confined to the Tower and so she was morose and anxious and tiresome. Elizabeth longed to spend more time with Henry. Already he was taking his position as future King of England seriously. He had with him his father's book, the *Basilikon Doron*—a dissertation on the behaviour that was considered appropriate for the heir to the throne.

God gives not Kings the style of Gods in vain, it began
For on his Throne his Sceptre do they sway. . . .

As Henry had already absorbed nearly all of this extraordinary
volume, he was determined that his young sister should learn it.
The *Basilikon Doron* embraced every subject from religion to
marriage; the use of language and the use of leisure.

"In your prayers," it went on, "be neither over strange with God,
like the ignorant common sort that prayeth nothing but out of
books, nor yet over homely with him, like some of our vain
Pharisaical puritans, that think they rule him upon their
fingers.

"In your language be plain, honest natural, comely, clean,
short . . ." it continued.

When writing of sport; football was banned but "the exercises
that I would have you use," King James wrote, "although, but
moderately, not making a craft of them, are running, leaping,
wrestling, fencing, dancing, and playing at the Catch. And the
honourablest and most commendable games that ye can use are
games on Horseback."

To please Henry, Elizabeth absorbed as much of it as she could.
Her willingness to learn was one way of holding his attention.
Flattered by his sister's adoration, Henry reciprocated with kindness. He began to think her not such a baby after all, but someone he
could talk sensibly to. Moreover she was amusing and vivacious,
which he was not, and he found her company refreshing.

When at last they reached London, Elizabeth stayed in Whitehall
just long enough to be held up by her unusually devoted father
in front of his courtiers and told that one day she would outdo her
mother in beauty. This had not pleased Queen Anne, whose
precarious state of health during the last few years had robbed her
almost entirely of the pink and white complexion which had been
her sole claim to beauty. She was relieved when her young daughter
was despatched to Oatlands with Henry. This enabled them to visit
Windsor the following April to watch the St. George's Day
celebrations, and then Elizabeth was taken further out of harm's

way, to the quiet domesticity of Coombe Abbey, in Warwickshire.

It was at Coombe Abbey that Elizabeth spent the formative years of her youth. It was the home of her new guardians, the Haringtons who had been appointed in October. Lady Kildare had been dismissed for her husband, Lord Cobham, had been found guilty of plotting against King James. Coombe Abbey was a beautiful place. Cloistered and surrounded by pastures and woodlands, it seemed to belong to a different age, away from the troubles of the present one. Oak and velvet dominated the furniture and beneath the large window of Elizabeth's bedroom were flowerbeds with a myriad of flowers. Stretching beyond were expanses of green and parkland, box hedges and lavender, bordering gravel paths.

The Haringtons were excellent guardians and Elizabeth's education perfectly equipped her to be what her father described as a "truly wise" princess. In effect she had her own court with footmen, grooms of the bed-chamber and so on, but, although it was designed for her, there were other children living at Coombe Abbey, who were treated almost identically to Elizabeth. Of these Anne Dudley, a niece of the Haringtons, was Elizabeth's closest friend. Together they rode through the parkland; played and shared lessons.

Their education was enlightened, in tune with the new scientific age proclaimed by James's Chancellor, Lord Bacon. Lord Harington was a born teacher. "If she took notice of the beauty of the sun, moon, or stars, the system was immediately explained to her," one of Elizabeth's companions wrote, "By these means she was freed from the fears which our sex was generally subject to, in those days when comets were looked upon as omens of good or bad fortune, and every star was thought by many to have an influence over their destiny; but Lord Harington, who was a good astronomer, and natural philosopher made us sensible that the stars were created for much nobler purposes, than to dance attendance on any single human creature." He would then go on to explain the laws of Copernicus and to illustrate his talk by allowing the children to peer through his famous telescope.

Her education was comprehensive. History, geography, theology, natural history, languages and music were all taught entertainingly. Elizabeth's music master was Dr. John Bull, the man who is supposed to have composed the national anthem. She had her own zoo, which comprised the smallest of each species of animal. She also kept various birds, some of which lived on an island in the centre of a lake at Coombe Abbey. According to one of Elizabeth's companions "the first orders she gave about it [the island] were, to have a little thatched building, which was in it rendered commodious within, for the dwelling of a poor widow and her children, who had been recommended to her charity and who, she intended should live in it, and take care of the different sort of fowls that were kept there." Along similar lines an old man was chosen to look after the birds in Elizabeth's aviary. "The top of this was round," wrote the same girl, "with coloured glass, that looked, at a little distance, like rough emeralds and rubies seemingly the produce of a rock overgrown with moss, which formed the back and roof of the aviary; the rest was enclosed with a net of gilt wire; within were many bushes, for birds to perch upon; and water falling continually from the artificial rock, into a shallow marble basin, in which the pretty feathered inhabitants drank and bathed at pleasure and recesses were made in the rock for them to build their nests in." If Elizabeth wanted a bird which could not survive the climate, Lord Harington would take infinite trouble to find one and have it stuffed and set up in the wood in a house appropriate to its country of origin. From that she would learn not only about the bird, but also about the architecture of the country it had come from.

Cunningly devised maps and illustrated pieces of paper, like playing cards, were used to teach history. Lord Harington would shuffle them and then tell the children to arrange them in chronological and dynastic order.

By the time Elizabeth was twelve she was fluent in several languages and imbued with a thorough understanding of the Protestant religion. She was not very musical and she did not enjoy needlework. However, she was an excellent rider and her knowledge did justice to the fact that she was the daughter of the professedly most learned king in Christendom. Already she was amusing and easily amused; popular and, unlike her father, very generous.

It was this generosity which stopped her, in Lord Harington's eyes, from being the ideal princess. She did not seem to comprehend the rudiments of domestic finance. She enjoyed giving presents and was quite unable to control her personal expenditure. Having found employment for various local people and financed them with her own allowance, she now wanted to start a school to educate local children. It was quite out of the question, Lord Harington told her; where was the money to come from? He might well ask, since whatever was spent over and above the Princess's allowance came out of his pocket and in fact he was seriously in debt as a result. When Lord Harington, scolded her for overspending, Elizabeth would burst into a flood of repentant tears and do it again. When King James occasionally came to see her, it would be her lack of thrift for which he criticised her. But on the whole it was an easy life. The days were spent in lessons, riding and walking in the grounds, and the evenings, according to her friend, "were generally taken up with music or dancing, and twice in the week, the children of all the nobility and gentry in the neighbourhood were admitted to her Company."

When she could find time Elizabeth would write letters. It was something for which she had an aptitude. Despite the conventional formalities, they sounded sincere and never stilted. "I will ever endeavour to equal you," she would write earnestly to Henry, "esteeming the time happiest when I enjoyed your company, and desiring nothing more than the fruition of it again."

She wrote, because King James had told her to, to the learned, but, according to the Venetian ambassador, "not very beautiful" Arabella Stuart, who lived in reduced circumstances in Blackfriars. Sometimes she wrote to Sir Walter Raleigh, whom Prince Henry visited in the Tower and who chivalrously described Elizabeth as "the precious jewel of this kingdom". Of course she wrote to her parents. Her letters, beautifully written, were elaborately tied with floss-silk. Normally she wrote of her affection, obedience and love. Once she sent a poem.

This is joy, this true pleasure,
If we best things make our treasure,
And enjoy them at full leisure,
Evermore in richest measure.

God is only excellent,
Unto him our love be sent,
Whose desires are set or bent
On aught else, shall much repent.

That I hereon meditate,
That desire, I find (though late)
To prize Heaven at higher rate,
And these pleasures vain to hate.

In fact very little ever happened at Coombe Abbey and so trifling (and not so trifling) incidents became enlarged in the minds of its inhabitants. One of these occasions was when a man called Massy, who staged pageants and whose services had been rejected by the Coventry Corporation because they were expensive, announced to the Corporation that in two days Lord Harington and the Princess Elizabeth would be coming to watch his play being performed in Coventry. This was totally untrue, as the Corporation soon discovered, but it did galvanize them into extending an overdue invitation to Elizabeth at Coventry at a later date and entertaining her.

More significant was the Gunpowder Plot of 1605. While Guy Fawkes was failing to blow up the Houses of Parliament, and King, Lords and Commons with them, another contingent of conspirators, feigning a hunting expedition, uneasily waited on Dunmore Heath, which was only ten miles from Coombe Abbey. When they received the signal, they intended to abduct Elizabeth and eventually put her on the throne as their puppet. They would have preferred Elizabeth's infant sister, Mary, who, as it turned out, only lived for a short time, or her brother, Charles; but as both those children were now in London, it would have been extremely difficult to abduct them.

As it was they did not abduct Elizabeth either. Although Lord Harington was given only a few hours' warning of the plot, he took her to Coventry and the people there promised to guard her with their lives. It never came to that. The conspirators were arrested, tried and executed and Elizabeth was soon back at Coombe Abbey. "What a Queen should I have been by this means?" she asked Lord Harington, "I had rather have been with my royal father in Parliament House than wear his Crown on such conditions." Being a Stuart the "conditions" were particularly repugnant to her. "Kings are justly called gods," her father, with his bandy legs and halting speech, had written confidently, "for that they exercise a manner or resemblance of Divine power upon earth; for if you will consider the attributes to God you shall see how they agree in the person of a King."

It was a doctrine which his daughter would never dispute. Nor would the writer of one of the many letters which King James received congratulating him on his escape. It was from Frederick, the young son of the Elector Palatine. "A wicked conspiracy," he described it, which must have come "from the direct agency of Anti-Christ."

The Gunpowder Plot was the chief topic of conversation at Coombe Abbey for the next six months and by the time the excitement had died down, Elizabeth had something else to think about. She was allowed to go to the Court for a short time during the stay in England of her uncle, King Christian of Denmark. Elizabeth loved the Court and all that went with it. The yeoman of the guard, all in glittering and colourful uniforms; the 200 sergeants at arms; the esquires of the body; standard-bearers; harbingers; singers; viol players; harriers and a rebeck player. Even the food at the banquets, shaped in curious patterns, immensely rich and varied, held her spellbound. And then there were the masques. Inigo Jones was responsible for the scenery, costumes and properties. Ben Jonson often contrived the scripts, replete with mythological figures and royal compliments. Even the bizarre delighted her. On one occasion she went with King Christian and Henry to watch a bear which had devoured a child and which King James had sentenced to be killed by a lion, defending itself successfully against the lion and eight mastiffs.

Diplomatically, however, the visit of King Christian was a failure. He left England early and Elizabeth had to return to Coombe Abbey. During the time she had spent in London, her admiration for Henry had increased. By now he was gathering his own courtiers around him. He was a good tennis player, an excellent horseman, fencer and golfer. According to Sir Charles Cornwallis, his pursuits at this time also included "hawking, hunting, running at the ring, leaping, riding of great horses, dancing, fencing, tossing the pike." Francis Bacon said of him he "was fond of antiquity and art: and a favourer of learning though rather in the honour he paid it than the time he spent upon it. . . . In body," he also observed, "he was strong and erect, of middle height, his limbs gracefully put together, his gait king-like, his face long and somewhat lean . . . resembling his sister as far as a man's face can be compared with that of a very beautiful girl. . . . His forehead bore marks of severity, his mouth had a touch of pride; and yet when one penetrated beyond these outworks, and soothed him with due attention and reasonable discourse, one found him gentle and easy to deal with." He was staunchly Protestant and consciously strove to be perfect. Elizabeth thought he was perfect and she was delighted when it became clear that there was no-one he cared for more than herself. "My affection is most tender unto you," he wrote once, "so there is nothing I wish more than that we might be in one company for many respects whereof you yourself may consider. But I fear that there be other considerations which maketh the Kings Majestie to think otherwise."

There was no getting away from the truth. Elizabeth's education, in her father's view at any rate, must come first. King James insisted that nearly another two years must be spent at Coombe Abbey.

The time was spent plesantly enough, but Elizabeth, dressed in adult clothes, watching her fluffy pet birds banging their wings against the oaken bars of their cage felt a new affinity with them.

She longed to graduate to Whitehall.

CHAPTER TWO

In 1608 King James allowed Elizabeth to move to Kew with the Haringtons. Once she was there, he took very little notice of her. By now he was besotted with Robert Carr, the young fairhaired man who continually lolled on his arm and who had first caught his attention by falling from a horse during a tilting match. Carr was one in a long line of favourites who influenced King James, against his better judgement, throughout his life. Henry disapproved of Carr and also, less overtly, of his father's coarse jokes. Elizabeth shrugged her shoulders. There were better things to do than worry about her father's sense of humour. Besides she was developing a fairly robust sense of humour herself. She needed it in the Jacobean Court. King James' personal habits were no better than his personal morals. He changed favourites, it was generally agreed, more frequently than he changed his clothes. Moreover, he encouraged financial corruption.

England had not turned out to be the land of milk and honey King James had expected. He had come to England during a period when commodity prices were rising on the one hand and on the other it was difficult to increase the revenues due to the Crown. Moreover, Queen Elizabeth had left debts which had to be paid and King James was not prepared to economise. He was in desperate need of cash and began to trade in monopolies and patents to fill his coffers. It did not take long for the words which had greeted King James in England: *Hail, mortal god*! *England's true joy*! *great king*, to sound unmelodious to English ears. They were not interested in the peace he had recently concluded with Spain, the excuses of his past, his learning. Even his moralising was derided. Surely it was only his tiresome Scots pedantry that regarded the new fashion of smoking as making "canker and venom".

Besides the omens were against him, and to the ordinary people that mattered. His coronation had been marred by an outbreak of the plague and a comet that had seared across the sky. His eldest son, on whom popular affection really rested, had not shed his milk-teeth, which was regarded as a symptom presaging early death. In 1605 disease was so rife in England that it was a miracle even to be able to get tallow off the sheep's carcases. King James was blamed even for this.

He didn't realise how unpopular he was becoming, or that other people had as pressing financial difficulties as he had. Up and down the country he went, demanding hospitality which was only grudgingly given by the nobility, who were hard-pressed by the rising cost of food. With him came his entourage, and with them, wherever they went, came disease.

Queen Anne was only marginally less unpopular than her husband. She treated England as a playground, indulging herself in masques and pageantry and gave the mistaken, but alarming impression that she might become a Roman Catholic. Moreover, foolishly, she was openly pro-Spanish. She didn't appreciate the peculiar relationship England had with Spain at this time: based partly on envy, partly on disgust at their extravagance and partly on fear. It wasn't long ago that the great Spanish Armada had been in English coastal waters and there had been a genuine fear that, like south and central America, the West Indies, the Philippines and parts of Italy, England would in effect become a Spanish colony, her riches being squandered in the Palace of the Escurial in Madrid.

One of the few redeeming features of the new monarch, in his subjects' eyes, was the fact that he had three presentable children. The youngest, Charles, it was true, had an impediment in his speech and an innate weakness in his legs which aroused pity rather than admiration, but his own remorseless efforts to overcome his disabilities were respected. Moreover he was so obviously well-intentioned that it was impossible to dislike him. His touching feelings towards his eldest brother, indicating no trace of jealousy, would, in themselves, have won him popularity.

"Sweet brother," Charles had once dictated adoringly, "I will give anything that I have to you; both my horses, and my books, and my pieces, and my crossbows or anything that you would have."

The English public idolised Henry. How could they do otherwise. According to his treasurer, Sir Charles Cornwallis, he was "of a comely, tall middle stature, [about 5ft 8in] of a strong, straight, well-made body (as if nature in him had showed all her cunning) with somewhat broad forehead, and a small waist, of an amiable, majestic countenance, his hair of an auburn colour, long-faced, and broad forehead, a piercing grave eye, a most gracious smile, with a terrible frown, courteous, loving and affable, his favour, like the sun indifferently seeming to shine upon all." He had brought a breath of fresh air into the Jacobean Court, a revival of a more chivalrous age.

> ... *Break, you rusty doors*, Ben Jonson wrote,
> *That have so long been shut, and from all shores*
> *Of all the world come knighthood, like a flood*
> *Upon these lists. . . .*

Henry was also musical, particularly enjoying the sound of the "trumpet and the drum". He was eager to patronise the arts. His father encouraged him and bought Lord Lumley's vast and comprehensive library for him. Authors were already dedicating their books to him. Clement Cotton's translation of Calvin's *A Commentary upon the Prophecy of Isaiah* was dedicated to Elizabeth as well. Henry was more interested in Raleigh's monumental *History of the World* which Sir Walter was busy re-writing in order to include the history of the Persians, the Greeks and the Romans at Henry's request.

Not everyone, however, unreservedly admired Henry. His courtiers and his father found him difficult at times. If Henry heard his friends swearing he would impose a fine on them which would be given to charity. A chance visitor would often be surprised to find the Prince strutting around in military garb, rehearsing military manoeuvres. On one occasion he had sent one of his servants to inspect the French fortifications at Calais. Why, King James wanted to know? There was no need for military maneouvres or for espionage. Wasn't his whole foreign policy aimed at sustaining peace? In every way King James felt that Henry opposed him. On his policy of appeasement with Spain; on his morals. Worse still he so blatantly supported Sir Walter Raleigh whose Sherbourne estate James had confiscated on the pretext that a phrase was missing from a legal document. He had then made it over to Carr. In all his dealings with Raleigh, King James had been petty and he knew it. Obviously it made him despise the man more. "None but my father," Henry had said, "would keep such a bird in a cage." What was the underlying meaning, James would ask himself? Was there an underlying meaning? He was becoming almost afraid of Henry. He dared not admit to himself the real irony—that Henry was following the *Basilikon Doron* to the letter. Here was the ideal Prince he had planned for and he didn't much like the result. Now that he wanted Henry to marry the Spanish Infanta, for instance, Henry responded that " two religions should not lie in the same bed". Had not James once written in a literary style which now eluded him "beware to marry one not of your own religion".

It was Henry's idea that he should be invested as Prince of Wales in 1610. It turned out to be an undistinguished occasion. Money as usual was short, and King James, for once, had agreed to economise. If he didn't, he had told himself, it might be mistaken for a coronation. He was becoming as coy about his heir as his predecessor had been about him.

There was the usual tilting match, fireworks and naval battle on the Thames. These were essential. So was the Lord Mayor's Show, which was watched from a "private gallery window" by the rest of the royal family. The pageantry culminated in the investiture ceremony. Bareheaded and dressed in purple velvet, Prince Henry was installed as Prince of Wales. After that Elizabeth played the part of a nymph of the Thames in her first masque, and King

James, having congratulated her of her performance, promptly forgot about the ceremony.

Henry did not. He now considered himself grown up. "His Highness," wrote Cornwallis, "being now absolute of himself did take up House with a full addition of high offices . . . making good and strict order . . . both above and below stairs, more like a grave, wise and ancient Counsellor, surveying, disposing and dispatching his affairs, than so young and great a Prince."

Elizabeth was less serious. People had begun to comment on her beauty; her flamboyance; her love of pageantry; her devotion to her friends; her kindness. They admired her long golden hair; her laughing eyes; her wit. They told her that one day she would be a queen. Nothing else would be good enough for her. It was true, she thought, as she looked at herself in the mirror. "Handsome, graceful, well-nourished," the French ambassador had said of her; but she promised to be more than that.

Other courtiers noticed, and found rather charming, the negligent way she dressed as though she didn't have time to bother about her appearance. It didn't matter. Her beauty was natural and not until much later did it have to rely on any contrivance.

She was continually occupied in the pursuit of happiness. Often she would not go to bed until two in the morning. It was exhausting for Lord Harington who usually acted as a chaperon and who sacrificed his private concerns in the interests of Elizabeth. He could not wait in person with the book of accounts, he wrote to Cecil once, because the Prince so often called for Elizabeth to ride with him that he needed to be constantly in attendance.

Elizabeth's horses did not take up all her time during the day. She had her private correspondence to see to, including petitions on behalf of her servants, her lessons and, more enjoyably, her own private barge on the Thames to visit. Henry was trying to establish himself as an authority on shipping. Elizabeth could often be found near the Thames with him watching the various ships that came and went from the docks. Whenever they could they would go and superintend the building of Prince Henry's own ship, the Venetian inspired *Prince Royal*. With lofty stem, elaborately carved and gilded it seemed more appropriate for a festival than the rough and tumble of the Channel. Henry was arranging a grand launching for it. Everyone had been invited and many people of importance came. But the boat, cumbersome, despite its beauty, slowly and ignominiously stuck in the silt of the Thames. Only long after dark was it finally floated. The crowds had gone by then. Henry's reign of perfection seemed to have ended. From now on little he did went well. Unlike his sister, he seems to have developed a streak of meanness which was talked about and a certain intensity which was not entirely attractive.

By now nearly every Court in Europe had heard about Elizabeths' beauty and charm. Ambassadors watched her, flattered her and sent reports home about her. Portraits of their masters arrived, along with extravaganzas about them—Gustavus Adolphus of Sweden; the Dauphin of France; the King of Spain; Prince Christian of Anhalt Bernberg and Elizabeth's kinsman, Ulric of Brunswick-Wolfenbuttel, both of whom had already tried for Arabella Stuart; Victor Amadeus, son of the Duke of Savoy, a pensioner of Spain; Frederick of the Palatinate. Elizabeth thought it would be the Dauphin. The French, who wanted Henry to marry one of their King's sisters, had been told he would not consider such a marriage unless Elizabeth was at the French court as well.

Queen Anne was encouraging Spain. But in the end it was the young Frederick of the Palatinate who came to woo Elizabeth.

1612 had been a bad year for the Stuarts. In May Cecil had died of dropsy, thus depriving King James of his most competent minister. During the summer of 1612 Henry had become ill. It was typhoid, perhaps the result of swimming in the Thames. The doctors however misdiagnosed it. People generally made light of the Prince's worsening condition, putting his paleness and thinness down to the weather and over-exertion But it was unlike Henry to complain and now he was continually rubbing his head and talking about a "giddy lumpish heaviness". But public attention was, for the time being, diverted from Henry to Frederick of the Palatinate. The young Elector arrived in London with a suite of 420 after a gruelling sea journey during which he had lost in a storm all the expensive clothes he had brought for his visit. Frederick of the Palatinate, First Elector of the Holy Roman Empire, looked younger than his age. At sixteen, and only three days older than Elizabeth herself, he was dark, with delicate features and a complexion unblemished by a recent attack of small-pox. He was fluent in several languages, although embarrassed by his ineptitude when it came to speaking English, and was an excellent horseman and a graceful dancer. His mother, the devout Louisa Juliana, daughter of William the Silent, had ensured that he had an extensive knowledge of Protestant theology. He was a Calvinist, who, as a small child had been brought up in the French-orientated Court at Heidelberg and then in Sedan with his maternal uncle, the Duc de Bouillon. It was Sedan that he loved. The woods surrounding the Castle, sheltering wild boar, wolves and deer; the streets narrow and twisting, always a bustle of activity; the enormous hall, which stretched the whole breadth of the Castle; these were memories to which he would often wistfully return. By sixteen Frederick had fixed ideas. He could understand no other religion but Calvinism and could imagine nothing that could taste more delicious than the strawberries which were grown in the greenhouses at Sedan or smell sweeter than the roses in the garden there. And yet he also had a sense of insecurity about him, a deep-rooted melancholy. There was no doubting that the Europe Frederick lived in was an uneasy place and that his position now, taking his dead father's position as a focus for German Protestantism, was an extremely awkward one.

The fact was that Frederick was not suited to the position of responsibility which had been thrust on him. He leant too heavily on his advisers Count Schomberg, the Prince of Anhalt and the Duc de Bouillon. Even his preoccupation with the loss of his clothes indicated his inability to cope. Perhaps he was nervous. The marriage agreement had already been drawn up, but King James could still retract. That would have been a terrible humiliation for Frederick. He was fundamentally proud and vulnerable and his relations, friends and subjects in the Palatinate had been astonished and delighted when King James had accepted the Duc de Bouillon's proposal that Frederick should marry Elizabeth. Frederick's

3. The Winter King and Queen.

4. Some of the children of Elizabeth and Frederick. (*above left*) Charles Louis; (*right*) Louise; (*centre*) Rupert; (*below left*) Henrietta Maria, and (*right*) Sophia.

rank, after all, for all his ancient lineage, was thoroughly eclipsed by King James's. King James, however, had his reasons. He intended to marry Henry to the Spanish Infanta, a project which would be difficult to justify to the English public since she was a Catholic. He felt that if Elizabeth was married to a Protestant then at least to some extent they would be appeased. Obviously Gustavus Adolphus of Sweden had higher rank than Frederick, but he was at war with King Christian of Denmark, Elizabeth's uncle, and so that match was out of the question. Frederick was the only real alternative. Besides King James had retorted once that "he doubted not but that his son-in-law should have the title of King within a few years". If that happened no-one could throw scorn on the match.

When Frederick first met the royal family, he addressed them in French. King James was kindly. Queen Anne was stiff. Henry was no more than polite. It had been a relief for Frederick to reach Elizabeth. Her eyes had not moved towards him as he came down the line of her relations. He bent down to kiss her dress and she curtsied to him, taking his hand in hers, gently lifting him up. For a moment Frederick paused. She was beautiful. The portraits had not lied. They had even underestimated her. No-one could entirely capture her laughing eyes, her diffident charm. He pulled himself together and spoke the formal words he had already rehearsed.

Elizabeth had fallen in love. Everything she had hardly dared to hope for, except the immediate likelihood of a throne, had come true. Throughout her life she had known that her marriage would be a pawn in her father's diplomacy. She might have had the King of Spain, who was eighteen years older than she and a widower. Instead she had someone of her own age, who shared her interests and whose only ambition now seemed to be to please her. With him Elizabeth grew more beautiful, charming, ebullient and witty and became so indulgent a companion to him that Frederick's boyishness quickly began to develop into manliness. She even began to care about her appearance and took to taking milk baths, which her father regarded as an unnecessary extravagance.

Moreover Frederick was interesting to talk to. Elizabeth knew hardly anything about the Palatinate with its fertile plains and its palaces, until Frederick boasted about them to her. She was fascinated to learn how Frederick's grandmother, Charlotte de Bourbon, had been put into a convent by her cruel father, never to see her mother again, and how she had been released; found her way to Sedan and eventually married William the Silent. The Castle of Bouillon, he told Elizabeth, and been pawned by Godfrey de Bouillon in order to finance the first Crusade and arguments still continued as to whether or not it had been properly redeemed. No-one was quite certain who owned it. Frederick confided his penchant for everything Italian and he told her of his recent visit to Vienna to watch the inauguration of the new Emperor, Matthias. He spoke about the mad Emperor Rudolph and the difficulties he had had in Prague, with the descendants of those who had followed Jan Hus against Rome over a century before the Protestant Reformers. Elizabeth would urge him to tell her more. Frederick had never before had such an attentive audience. She was perpetually, almost feverishly, excited. It was almost disquieting, as though she had a premonition of what was to come.

It was in the autumn that people really began to show concern about Henry's state of health and by then it was too late. During the summer he had developed the habit of brushing his brow with his hand, as though half-distracted. Sometimes he would walk late by the river in the moonlight which "many suspected", as one observer put it, "because the dew then falling, did him small good". He had complained of "a cold, leafy, drowsiness in his head", and his doctors had treated him for violent nosebleeds.

All this was made more ominous by the fact that Henry had stopped discussing his future and begun ordering the payment of pensions for his servants. Occasionally he would have a sudden spurt of energy and he might ride as far as Nottingham and then down to London again with half the ordinary breaks.

Late in October he insisted on wearing nothing on top of his shirt while playing tennis with Frederick Henry of Holland at Whitehall. The next day he had developed a chill. His doctors advised him to stay in bed, but he ignored their advice and got up to listen to a sermon, which turned out to be about mortification and preparation for death. At first no-one realised how appropriate that sermon had been. Henry stayed in bed consuming a "sharp, tart, cordial and cooling Juleps, prepared with all kinds of cordials and antidotes possible, his broths and jellies being with the same care ordained . . . [and] a purgation of senna pod, and rhubarb infused in cordial and cooling liquors, with syrup of roses." On the eighth day of his illness, Elizabeth and Frederick were told that he was well enough for them to visit him, which they did.

It was on the tenth day that it became clear that he was dying. It was suspected that his disease was infectious and Elizabeth was forbidden to see him. In vain she tried disguising herself as a page and bribing the attendants to gain admission. Nothing was achieved and his illness continued to get worse. During his last hours from behind closed doors, Elizabeth heard Henry crying out again and again, "Where is my dear sister?" He bequeathed her a chain set with diamonds, and anxiously ordered that certain letters should be destroyed.

The doctors purged him with the blood of newly killed cocks and pigeons and the infection spread. Sir Walter Raleigh sent a specially concocted brew ominously accompanied with the assurance that it "would certainly cure him or any other of a fever, except in case of poison". But by the time it had been tested to make sure that it was not itself poison, Henry was dead.

None of his family had been with him. King James had fled to Theobalds and Queen Anne was at Somerset House. Elizabeth had done her best, but failed. Now she gave way to hysterical grief.

Rumours immediately began to circulate. The Howards, old enemies of the Prince, were suspected of poisoning him with the help of his Chamberlain, who practised chemical experiments. The Spanish, whom Henry had opposed openly, were also believed to be implicated in some way. Even James was said to have had a hand in it, although anyone who had seen his bewildered grief-stricken face and understood that it had been his pathological fear of death rather than a feeling of guilt which had driven him to Theobalds, would not have credited that.

Farewell the Joy of King and mother,
Farewell Eliza's dearest brother,—a rhymster wrote at the time.

There was only one person for Elizabeth to turn to and it was on Frederick that she gave full vent to her grief.

Young Frederick of Royal Line, the same rhymster wrote,
Of Casimirs, who on the Rhine
To none are second said to be
For valour, Bounty, Pietie.

CHAPTER THREE

For a month Henry lay in state in St. James's Palace. Through rooms, all draped in black, passed a constant stream of curious and bereaved visitors.

Elizabeth was absorbed in her grief. Nothing seemed to dispel it. Frederick read her the passages from the Bible which he remembered his mother had found most consolation from after the death of his father, but he knew that Elizabeth longed only to hear Henry's halting voice with its faintly Scottish accent reading them. It was tiresome to have such an irreproachable rival. Again and again Elizabeth went over the conversations she had had with Henry, his strictures on the Roman Catholic religion and his belief in the divine right of kings. Hour after hour, looking dully out of her new apartments in the Cockpit, she eschewed any comfort but from the fact that she would carry on Henry's work and uphold the Protestant cause. She urged Frederick to do the same. It was the only thing, she confided to him as he sat anxiously beside her, that gave her any hope of happiness. There was an unnatural fervour in her voice, too much earnestness for someone who was so young and untried.

Frederick tried to comfort her. When she asked for promises that he would follow up Henry's work, supporting the Protestant cause and never swerving from that aim, he gave them willingly, convincingly and ill-advisedly.

In return Elizabeth began to rely entirely on him. Only Frederick seemed capable of understanding her grief. The twelve-year-old Charles, who spent most of his time with her, was too young, and King James, who was already showing signs of premature senility, was too old. Moreover, the financial implications of Henry's death had distracted him from the horrid reality.

He could not admit to himself that Henry's death would not have serious financial consequences. In fact the reverse was true. Had Henry married early, as his father had hoped, and produced within a dozen years, as Sir Walter Raleigh had anticipated, twelve hungry princes and princesses, he would have proved extremely expensive. Instead King James chose to dwell monotonously on the fact that Frederick's followers would have to be housed and fed much longer than he had anticipated. When his treasurer, Sir Julius Caesar, reminded him that the royal debt now stood at £500,000 James alluded to Frederick. The weary Treasurer suggested certain economies: abolishing the Jewel Tower, abating building; but in the King's eyes the only acceptable solution was the despatch of the German entourage home, and perhaps the suitor as well.

That roused Elizabeth from her grief. Having lost her brother, she was not prepared to part with Frederick as well. Frederick himself exerted all his charm on King James. Before Henry was buried he was whisked down to James' hunting lodge at Royston while Elizabeth waited anxiously in London. What peculiar shift of policy, she wondered, might now appeal to her father? What setback might occur? To her her father had always seemed unpredictably changeable and never more so than now.

At the funeral Frederick was allocated an important part, but there was still talk of his going. He was under perpetual scrutiny. A suitable husband for the King of England's only daughter might be thoroughly unsuitable as the consort of a Queen of England. Charles, after all, was still frail. He might not survive his father.

And then, capricious as always, King James decided that he could stand the atmosphere of mourning no longer and what was needed was a wedding. On 18 December 1612, he invested Frederick with the Order of the Garter in Henry's place. The ceremony was unregally conducted from King James' bed, where he was confined with a sore toe.

On 27 December they became officially betrothed. The ceremony took place in the Banqueting House at Whitehall. Frederick was dressed in purple velvet and Elizabeth observed half-mourning in a dress of black satin with a large white feather in her hair. Queen Anne used her gout as an excuse for not attending. Her absence was hardly noticed.

Elizabeth had resolved to shake off her grief and she did her best. She actually laughed during the ceremony at the strange French translation of the service and people noticed the old glint of amusement in her eyes when the next day half the Court had adopted her idea of wearing white feathers. It was characteristic of her that she did not display her sadness. Elizabeth never dwelt obsessively on the past or, for that matter, on the future. Now she decided to enjoy the preparations for the wedding.

That was not too difficult when she was with Frederick. She could tease him and cajole him more forthrightly than she had ever done Henry. Her "nigger duckling" she called him, and she plagued him about his height.

He was intensely happy. Now that his position was secure he became more confident. On New Year's Day he had intended to give presents to everyone including the servants. King James, who was always afraid that his underlings might be prospering too well from being in his service, put a stop to that. Frederick therefore lavished his generosity on the royal family. "A rich chain of diamonds, a tiara for her head all of diamonds, two very rich pendant diamonds for her ears and above all two pearls, for bigness, fashion and beauty esteemed the rarest that are found in Christendom", were the presents he gave Elizabeth. They were less imaginative than the parrot she was given by Prince Henry's old friend, Thomas Roe, but more durable, and in later years when Elizabeth was selling most of her jewellery (and even the horses she loved so much) she would not relinquish the pearls Frederick had given her when the strange ebony of those gems had toned in so well with the mourning court, uniting the only two loves of her life.

The ensuing weeks were spent almost entirely in the public eye. Whether Elizabeth was being painted wearing an uncomfortable farthingale, with a fashionable high stiff-laced collar round her neck and an enormous rosette at her shoulder, or watching fireworks from a barge on the Thames, or even walking in the gardens of Denmark House, everyone knew about it. Even the fact that nearly every night she lost small sums to her father at cards was generally known. The inevitable performances of masques and plays, the hunting parties and the banquets almost entirely filled Elizabeth's days until her wedding.

The date had been fixed for St Valentine's Day 1613. The wedding was to take place in the Chapel Royal at Whitehall and, because there was so little space, no-one under the rank of Baron, except the three Lords Justices, could attend. Foreign ambassadors were as usual haggling over matters of protocol. The ambassadors of France and Venice were being particularly tiresome. They insisted on sitting on chairs, which were so scarce that even Prince Charles had not been allocated one, rather than stools at the ceremony. More ominously, the Spanish ambassador pleaded illness as an excuse for not attending and the Holy Roman Emperor firmly refused to send a representative.

Throughout the country broadsheets were being distributed and pedigrees produced to show that Frederick and Elizabeth were mutually descended from Edward II and that Elizabeth was descended from Banquo and from John of Gaunt. Some "proved" Frederick's "direct descent" from Charlemagne.

The prospect of the marriage even aroused the attention of the unfortunate Arabella Stuart, with whom Elizabeth had corresponded so conscientiously as a child. Now she was incarcerated in the Tower because not only had she married without the King's consent, but she had married the one man least likely to gain it. Her husband was William Seymour, son of Edward, Lord Beauchamp, and thus a claimant to the English crown. Were they to have children, these would represent a real threat to the House of Stuart. Arabella had succeeded once in escaping from the Tower. Her husband had got away to the Continent, but she had been recaptured. James intended to make quite sure of her this time so the four gowns she had ordered in anticipation of the wedding had to be dismantled and Arabella, with her last glimpse of freedom thwarted, relapsed into madness and soon died.

Elizabeth's circumstances could not have been more different. "Thou that mak'st a day of night, Goddess excellently bright," Ben Jonson wrote of her. John Donne wrote his poem "Epithalamium" for her.

> *Up then fair Phoenix Bride, frustrate the sun,*
> *Thy self from thine affection*
> *Takest warmth enough, and from thine eyes*
> *All lesser birds will take their Jollity.*
> *Up, up, fair Bride, and call,*
> *Thy stars, from out their several boxes, take*
> *Thy rubies, pearls, and diamonds forth, and make*
> *Thy self a constellation, of them all,*
> *And by their blazing signify,*
> *That a great Princess falls, but doth not die;*
> *Be thou a new star, that to us portends*
> *Ends of much wonder; and be thou those ends.*
> *Since thou dost this day in new glory shine,*
> *May all men date records, from this thy Valentine.*

Even William Shakespeare was busy adjusting his play, *The Tempest*, so that a masque "a contract of true love to celebrate" could be fitted into it involving the presenting of gifts to Frederick and Elizabeth and expressing the usual hopes for a productive marriage.

> *Honour, riches, marriage, blessing,*
> *Long continuance, and increasing,*
> *Hourly joys be still upon you!*
> *June sings her blessings on you.*
> *Earth's increase, foison plenty,*
> *Barns and garners never empty,*
> *Vines and clust'ring bunches growing,*
> *Plants with goodly burden bowing;*
> *Spring come to you at the farthest*
> *In the very end of harvest.*
> *Scarcity and want shall shun you,*
> *Ceres' blessing so is on you.*

Elizabeth certainly enjoyed reading flattering accounts of her beauty and wit and charm, but she was less certain that she liked the continual suggestions that she should have a child "in the very end of harvest", as Shakespeare had put it. More directly Henry Peacham wrote a particularly uninspired verse hoping:

> *That one day we may live to see,*
> *A Frederick Henry on her knee . . .*

Elizabeth hoped that that "one day" was still a long way off.

The celebrations for the wedding began with a huge firework display on 11 February 1613. The punsters were in their element when the outline of a hart being chased flashed across the sky. That was followed by a dragon, spouting flames, and sporting hundreds of different coloured fireworks, which faded almost before their form had been discovered.

On Saturday there was a disastrous mock sea battle. Among the participants there were as many casualties as there would have been had the fight been genuine. Men were maimed and blinded and the spectators were bewildered and depressed.

On Sunday the wedding took place. People had traversed the appalling roads from the length and breadth of England to be there. Never before in their lives had a royal occasion promised to be so spectacular.

The ceremony began with a long procession which included the crown jewels, which King James felt needed an airing, and the royal family. After a detour so that the people could see them, Elizabeth and Frederick eventually entered the Chapel Royal.

They were surrounded by every emblem of good fortune: rosemary for fidelity; flowers of blue and yellow for honour and joy. Elizabeth's golden hair, which unfortunately had been plaited and "frizzed" according to the custom of the day, fell down her back and was crowned with a priceless coronet. Her face was radiant and fortunately it was that fact that the chroniclers noticed more than anything else; that "she was attired all in white" and her dress inset with heavy pearls and diamonds was secondary. In the tasteless Jacobean style, it incorporated yards of tightly folded material and did not do her justice. It was so heavy that she had to change out of it immediately after the ceremony. With the real texture of her hair and her slimness totally concealed she looked nearer forty than sixteen. It was only the animation in her eyes that indicated that this might not be a walking doll or a puppet, but an excited passionate young girl.

As for King James, an observer remarked critically: "The King methought was somewhat strangely attired in a cap and feather with a Spanish cape and a long stocking". The only remarkable fact about Queen Anne's attire was that her plain white satin dress was adorned with jewelry worth £400,000.

As Elizabeth entered the Chapel, followed by sixteen bridesmaids as a symbol of her age, she doffed her long gloves and dispensed with the bridesmaids. Because of the lack of space, only Lady Harington could escort her down the aisle.

Frederick followed, dressed in white satin and accompanied by sixteen noble bachelors who were extravagantly dressed in silver. He seemed preoccupied. Probably he was rehearsing his responses for the service. Four months in England had not made him fluent in the English language.

The service was long and unusual. For the first time a royal wedding was being performed according to the *Book of Common Prayer*.

Not everything, however, was left to the liturgy. When the service was over there was the usual pandering to public superstition. Ornamental rings were exchanged; there was drinking from a cup of muscadel. As far as they went, the omens seemed to work. The next day when James cross-questioned Frederick as to whether "he was his true son-in-law or no" he was satisfied that he was.

During the next few days the entertainments continued with torchlight processions by land and by water, tilting matches, and, inevitably, masques. There seemed to be no limit to Inigo Jones' inventiveness, for it was he who designed the sets and contrived the elaborate stage-effects. But King James found them irksome and on the third evening announced that if he saw another masque it would kill him. In the end he was persuaded merely to postpone the remaining performance.

Having safely deposited the jewels he had worn at the wedding, King James now began to worry about the expense of the festivities. On one occasion he managed to win some money from Frederick and his followers "upon a wager of running at the ring" to pay for a banquet. But the real solution demanded that he send some of the Germans home early and arrange for Elizabeth and Frederick to leave England as soon as possible. By the middle of March nearly £50,000 had been spent on the wedding and the celebrations. "We devise," wrote one observer, "all means we can to cut off expense and not without cause, being come ad fundum and to the very lees of our best liquor."

Only the Germans seemed to have any money. While Frederick and Elizabeth lingered in London, waiting for the ships which were to take them across the Channel to be refurbished, Frederick continued to ply Elizabeth with presents. On one occasion he gave her a magnificent French coach. He presented a similar one to his mother-in-law, hoping, no doubt, to win her approbation. Queen Anne, characteristically, accepted the present and then continued to refer to the proliferation of princes in Germany and to taunt Elizabeth by calling her "good wife Palsgrave", admittedly rather less vociferously than before.

At heart Queen Anne liked Frederick, but nothing could make her forget that he was a mere "Palsgrave". Elizabeth, she thought had let her down. As the wife of a king, the daughter of a king and the sister of a king, Queen Anne had expected, and indeed regarded it as her right, to be the mother of a queen. All the coaches in Christendom could not have diminished that feeling of disappointment.

But it was King James' attitude towards Frederick that most distressed Elizabeth. "Son, when I come into Germany I will promise not to importune you for any of your prisoners", had been the surly retort when Frederick had asked for the customary release of a prisoner as a mark of goodwill.

It was almost a relief when April came and they set off for Rochester. Among Elizabeth's entourage were three laundresses, a cup-bearer, Anne Dudley, and Lord and Lady Harington. A few days before Elizabeth had had to remind her father that the Haringtons had not been reimbursed for all their services to her. King James had grudgingly granted the right to coin brass farthings, which he knew would never cover the £30,000 which he owed. That cast a shadow over Elizabeth's leave-taking.

King James, Queen Anne and Prince Charles accompanied Elizabeth to Rochester. As they went, the crowds who wished Elizabeth goodbye murmured that it was very likely that she would soon return as Queen of England. Prince Charles was still physically weak and unlikely to live to maturity.

Elizabeth thought otherwise. Instinctively she felt that she would never see any of them again. Like Henry, they would be nothing but memories. She urged them to stay longer. Her heart, she declared, was "pressed and astounded". King James, however, felt her departure had been delayed long enough.

Queen Anne was the first to say goodbye. As usual where her daughter was concerned, she feigned more emotion than she felt. King James took the opportunity of exploiting Elizabeth's very real grief. He followed her on to the ship, which was to take the royal couple up the river and, with Elizabeth sobbing uncontrollably at his side, he extracted a promise from Frederick that she would take precedence over his mother, Louisa Juliana, at the Court of Heidelberg and always be treated as if she were a queen. It was a promise which was to cause far more trouble than it was worth.

Prince Charles was the only member of the royal family to display any great emotion at her going. He insisted on coming to Canterbury with Frederick and Elizabeth and there they spent a few idyllic days exploring the City.

Then a message came from King James demanding Charles's presence at the Order of the Garter ceremony. His presence was unnecessary, but the spell was broken and reluctantly he left them.

On 21 April 1613, Frederick and Elizabeth boarded the ship that was to take them to Holland. It was none other than the ill-fated *Prince Royal*, which had proved so troublesome to Henry during its launching. Unashamedly reliant on omens, several people had urged Elizabeth not to travel in it. She, however, insisted. As usual the ship was late in leaving. Five days passed until the weather was considered suitable for the journey.

As the English landscape slowly faded from view, Frederick consoled Elizabeth with the hope that she would soon return. In fact nearly half a century was to pass until she would cross the Channel again, weary and disenchanted, to find a very different England. But now the people waved to her from the shore; small boats followed the *Prince Royal* out to sea; the Union Jack (St Andrew's cross now joining that of St George) waved vigorously in the wind and 700 followers—opportunists as well as loyal servants—determined to make the journey in her wake.

Sir Henry Wotton caustically commented to his nephew that Elizabeth and Frederick had "put to sea some eight days after a book had been printed and published in London of her entertainment in Heidelberg, so nimble an age it is."

CHAPTER FOUR

When Frederick and Elizabeth had crossed the Channel, they set foot in a Europe which revolved around two weak figures: Austria and Spain. Spain's declining birthrate and ailing economy—through lack of policy—had not alleviated the traditional wariness of every court to her activities, and Austria remained imperious, like a Grande Dame expecting the homage which she felt, perhaps deservedly as long as she acted as a bulwark against the Turks, to be her intrinsic right. In the sidelines were Holland with its unashamed reliance on commerce, which was too successful not to arouse envy and Sweden under the brilliant and confident Gustavus Adolphus, longing to expand her territories. France had regained power and solvency under Henri IV and his great minister, Sully. Everybody said that the king had been planning an attack on the Empire in 1610, when he was assassinated by a fanatical monk. As France relapsed into a temporary anarchy of greedy grandees, the Hapsburgs were saved for the time being. It would be some time before an even more powerful state emerged under Richelieu.

It was not only the usual fear of dynastic territorial expansion which made the Europe which Elizabeth was about to travel through an uneasy place. Religion, the conflict between Calvin's "chosen few" doctrine of predestination, Luther's Protestantism and the Roman Catholic Church, which vied in every Court, was intensifying. Nowhere was affected more than Germany. There the three religions sustained only the merest semblance of a truce.

The leader of the Catholic cause was the bigoted, but often deceptively good-natured, Ferdinand of Styria. Maximilian, Duke

37

of Bavaria, was also a fervant Catholic. Both these princes longed
for the whole of Germany to be embraced by their faith. In 1608
the Emperor and Maximilian of Bavaria had suppressed Protestantism in Donauwörth. This had so shocked German opinion, for
Donauwörth was a Free City outside Imperial jurisdiction, that the
Protestant princes—Lutherans and Calvinists—formed the Evangeli-
cal Union to protect themselves. The following year the Catholics
formed the Catholic League with Maximilian at its head. Now both
sides waited, poised for inevitable conflict. But as the spark which
was to ignite the fuse, Frederick himself, led his bride through
Europe, for a moment the tension lulled and the energies expended
themselves in other, less harmful, pursuits.

Their ship, with its carved and gilded stern, was intercepted near
the coast of Holland by Frederick's uncle, Prince Maurice of
Nassau. He was small, fat and jovial and Elizabeth liked him
immediately. He in turn appreciated her enthusiasm for the
volleys of great shot and the display of fireworks that greeted them
when they landed at Flushing.

The United Provinces—Holland was only one of them—were a
new power in the world. But whereas until 1609 when a truce with
Spain had been concluded, they had been united by dangers
without, they were now disunited by the different factions within.
Religion was the paramount issue. The population was predominantly Calvinist in varying degrees and it was those varying degrees
which caused the controversy. King James was making himself
unpopular by interfering. His ambassadors had been sent to lecture
the States General, which was the governing body, on the finer
points of predestination as he saw them. He had failed to grasp how
fiercely independent the small new nation across the Channel was.
Having shaken off the Spaniards, they were hardly likely to accept
another outside influence. The sudden emergence of the Dutch
nation was due to her success in shipping, fishing, banking, industry,
insurance and overseas commerce. For a short time in the seventeenth century, Holland was so far ahead of its contemporaries in the
exercise of individual freedom, hygiene and commerce, that it
resembled Atlantis, even to sinking or rather declining in the end

almost without a trace. In 1613 Holland had not yet reached that Golden Age, but the busy activity at the port and the scrupulous cleanliness of the streets hinted at its potentialities.

King James's tiresome expostulations and the fact that the United Provinces were a republic did not in any way diminish his daughter's welcome. A stathouder was not the same thing as a king and, they greeted this king's daughter unreservedly and generously. They were also curious. They had never before seen so many trunks belonging to one person, or so many dresses. At every banquet, firework display, pageant and mock battle, Elizabeth wore a different dress. It was in entire contrast to the quiet sobriety of their own women. Frederick's mother, for instance, Louisa Juliana, had been born at Dort and had enjoyed a happy devout and unrestricted childhood in Holland. It had left her so unsophisticated that even now she was unable to come to terms with the formal (and inebriated) court at Heidelberg. She had urged her son to visit her birthplace during his journey home. And so obediently Frederick left Elizabeth for a short time to go there.

While Frederick was away Maurice took the opportunity of making himself as agreeable as possible to Elizabeth. It was flattering to be given so much attention by one with the reputation of being the foremost soldier in Europe. Moreover so much that he said seemed logical and wise. Her ideas were, as Henry's had been, firmly rooted in the well-being of the Protestant cause. It at times Maurice tried to convince Elizabeth of the merits of Calvinism, he at least did not press her too hard.

Other relations had by now arrived to greet her. Louise de Coligny, the remarkable third wife of William the Silent, had come from Paris with some French furniture to put in Elizabeth's room; Frederick Henry, the 29-year-old half-brother of Maurice, who had played that last fatal game of tennis with Henry; Elizabeth's cousin, Sophia of Brunswick-Wolfenbüttel, who was married to Count Ernest of Nassau-Dietz; and Emmanuel of Portugal. All were doing their utmost to make her happy and, although Frederick had by now gone ahead to Heidelberg, Elizabeth appeared to be constantly delighted by everything she saw. Every present she was given prompted such a burst of spontaneous enthusiasm from her that the Dutch were soon talking of her "noble behaviour" and the "great contentments" she gave "to all the beholders". A group of Dutch merchants presented her with sixteen beautifully worked tapestries, a bedroom suite brought all the way from China and an enormous dinner service. At Harlem she was given a cradle and some baby clothes and at Amsterdam, where she saw thirty cities from the top of a tower, she was given some gold plate.

In the excitement of it all she hardly noticed that there was very little music and tilting in Holland and that the flat dull landscape, only occasionally alleviated by sparse trees and domestic windmills, contrasted sharply with the faraway places in the sun the Dutch talked about and from which their merchants brought back damask linen, rare spices and porcelain.

By the time she had reached the border of Germany, everyone knew that she had shot three stags in one afternoon and that she thought Rhenen, a place on the Rhine near Arnheim, the prettiest spot in the world. Moreover she had touched the hearts of the Dutch people, normally so impenetrable and unyielding.

As she was leaving Holland, Elizabeth was presented by the States General with diamonds, pearl pendants, a huge needle inset with diamonds, tapestries, linen and china. At this point her father's ambassador, Lord Winwood, started on his homeward journey. When he arrived at Whitehall he had nothing but praise for Elizabeth and he was able to assure King James that in Holland, at least, England had a firm ally.

From Holland she passed into Germany. Here the entertainment was less lavish and it was more difficult to be diplomatic. The first part of the journey took them through the disputed Duchy of Jülich-Cleves. Only the assassination of Henri IV and the death of Frederick's father had stopped Catholics and Protestants going to war over it. As the Elector of Brandenburg was still quarrelling over it with the other claimant, the Count of Neuberg, a member of Frederick's family, the local inhabitants viewed Elizabeth's visit as inappropriate under the circumstances. Then a message came from the Archduke Albert, Governor of the Spanish Netherlands and his wife Isabella of Spain inviting her to stay at their castle. If Elizabeth had accepted that invitation she could have forfeited the goodwill she had gained in Holland. She therefore refused and thus antagonised Spain.

Elizabeth and her followers, whose number had now escalated to nearly 4,000, went on to Cologne, with its lovely Gothic Cathedral, which had been started in 1248 and was still uncompleted.

From here they went to Bonn where the Margrave of Brandenburg had organised a magnificent picnic with a view up the Rhine of dark forests whose huge pine trees seemed to surge from the river itself while the straggling rocks jutted out of the water. The whole scene was replete with history and legends. But Elizabeth was already feeling pangs of homesickness. Maurice and Frederick Henry were preparing to leave. Frederick was in Heidelberg preparing her welcome. He had dispatched the ship which was to take Elizabeth up the Rhine. It had been designed under his instructions. With the velvets, tapestries, silks, laurels, imitation marble columns and its figure on the stern responding to the movement of the boat representing Fate and its vicissitudes, it was far more splendid than the one which had taken them across the Channel.

At first Elizabeth was enchanted with the ship and the Rhineland scenery: the terraces, orchards and vineyards undulating in the distance and sometimes unexpectedly revealing a castle or a church where a group of peasants would be waving at the passing flotilla.

King James and Frederick had agreed that Bacharach, the home of the Lorelei legend, should be the dividing line between their financial responsibilities. However, as Elizabeth approached Bacharach, a message arrived from Frederick to say that there was an outbreak of the plague and she was to go to Gilsheim instead. He soon joined her and they continued their journey up the river. The lands they now passed through had once been the private estates of the Hohenstaufen emperors. Frederick II had given them to Frederick's family, the Wittelsbachs, four hundred years before.

Passing Oberwinter, a gorge opened out, to reveal the medieval town of Andernach on the right bank. They then carried on up the

Rhine, past the dark remains of volcanic eruptions, deserted castles and productive vineyards.

At each stop Elizabeth was expected to distribute presents. It was something she had not anticipated. Unfortunately she did not have the money to pay for them. Afraid of appearing ungenerous, she persuaded her jeweller to provide her with suitable presents on credit giving him a jewel as a "gage": "Upon these conditions," as she later wrote to her father, "that if your Majestie did not pay him for all those things that of necessity I was forced to take of him, to give away in my journey, he should have the said jewel till such time as I had paid him, for I had no money then to discharge so great a debt."

There was the further problem of her followers. Some had accepted their prearranged dismissal when they reached Gilsheim and left for home, but many more had somehow contrived to continue the journey into the Palatinate.

As the boat, relying on only one oar, continued its voyage up the river, Elizabeth began to find so much inactivity monotonous. The magnificence of the scenery had long ago ceased to divert her and she insisted on proceeding by land. For someone who was reputed to be considerate, it was a strange decision. Along the line of her original route pageants and displays had been organised at great expense. The local populations had probably thought of nothing during the last few weeks except the excitement of seeing their new Electress. Elizabeth, however, was not very imaginative. She liked giving to people she knew, or had heard about personally. The drudgery and dreariness of the peasants' way of life was something with which she had never come in contact. If she had understood it and in any way attempted to alleviate it, she would have been a very unusual seventeenth-century princess.

However her reception at her dower in Franckenthal must have given her some indication of what she had missed. Everyone was wearing either armour or their best clothes. The streets were strewn with flowers and the houses overhung with branches. There were statues of Elizabeth and Frederick and a throne which was draped and lighted similarly to the one which Solomon had sat on when he had entertained the Queen of Sheba. The following day there was a pageant-performance of the Siege of Troy. In short "she was joyfully received with an infinite concourse of people." By now Frederick had left her to be with his subjects when she entered Heidelberg.

The City of Heidelberg stood on the edge of the Neckar surrounded by hills and fertile plains. Frederick, more to impress her English entourage and indirectly King James, than Elizabeth herself, had arranged an enormous mock battle on the outskirts of the town. He had also organised a picnic, but the weather was so unsettled that that had to be cancelled. As Elizabeth entered Heidelberg she saw that like Franckenthal the streets were strewn with flowers. A thousand gentlemen on horseback came out to greet the young girl, who was dressed in a heavy gold farthingale and a high red hat. Frederick asked her to mount a horse herself and ride into the town on it, but Elizabeth, who in fact was three months pregnant, refused. Instead she announced that she preferred to travel in a coach, which was open on either side so that the people could see her.

As she passed over the bridge the fishermen played games to amuse her, spiking a revolving turret with lances and often falling into the water in the process, and shooting a goose which was attached to a floating scaffold.

At one point, as she was moving through the main street of the town, a crown, which would have alighted on her head had she been riding as Frederick had suggested, dropped on to the carriage, only strangely prophetically to be hastily hauled up again. When her carriage stopped, a child presented her with a basket of flowers and rare fruit which had been grown in the Castle orangery. Elizabeth, feeling that she deserved some refreshment, ate the fruit there and then.

There were volleys of great shot as she approached Heidelberg Castle, with its huge rooms commemorating the traditions of the House of Wittelsbach right back to the time of Otto I, its celebrated library full of rare books, its allegorical tapestries and its Jethel Tower. Every age had made its own addition to the Castle. An extension had been added in one place, an arch, some statues in another. But as Elizabeth entered, it was the sun that dominated, shining forcefully across the red brick.

Frederick lifted Elizabeth from the coach and led her to where his mother was standing. Elizabeth welcomed her with such enthusiasm that afterwards the older woman announced that she had been quite taken aback. He had then introduced her to the two Duchesses of Zweibrücken, his sister and mother-in-law; and his two unmarried sisters, Charlotte and Catherine. Behind them stood a vast line of noble men and women, in strict order of heraldic precedence.

On the following days there were more pageants and tournaments with complimentary allegories and more flowers. There was hunting as well and dancing. Soon the wiser among the inhabitants began to wonder if, after all, this beautiful young laughing Stuart might be robbing them in one week of the meagre prosperity which the Palatinate had achieved in the last fifty years.

CHAPTER FIVE

Perhaps it was King James' preoccupation with the customs of Spain which made him such a stickler on the question of precedence. Whatever it was, it no more enhanced his daughter's happiness than those tiresome Spanish farthingales (verdingales) or those rigid hairstyles supported by wires enhanced her beauty. The fashions from Spain were not King James' responsibility, but the question of precedence could have been resolved had King James been less concerned with theories and more with human relationships.

From the moment Elizabeth arrived in Heidelberg, full of hope and good intentions, it was inevitable that there would be friction between her and her mother-in-law. Louisa Juliana had not expected to be demoted in favour of her young daughter-in-law and Frederick should not have committed himself as he had. But had he had an alternative? He had been sent to England with specific instruction in no way to upset the English King. The English King had pressed him, at his most vulnerable, on the subject and Frederick had not dared to oppose him.

Now that Elizabeth was in Heidelberg she pleaded with her adviser, Count Schomberg, to find some way out of the impasse. Count Schomberg responded by reminding her of her duties to England. It was essential, he told her, that she should be treated as if she were a queen and as such take precedence over Frederick as well as his mother. That only made matters worse and the result was that Elizabeth and Frederick could never appear in public together.

The approbation Elizabeth had always received in Whitehall and Coombe Abbey was therefore changed to a feeling of distrust and friendlessness in the Heidelberg Court. Louisa Juliana, devout and self-sacrificing as she was, was also narrow-minded. She blamed the disagreement over who should precede whom into dinner and who should have the highest chair, entirely on Elizabeth. Her daughters, Charlotte and Catherine, naturally sided with their mother. They agreed with her when she accused Elizabeth of "levity", but probably for different motives.

Self-effacing by nature and more suited really to a nun's life than that of Electress-Dowager, Louisa Juliana did not envy Elizabeth her comparative sophistication or her ebullience. In fact she plainly disapproved. Elizabeth's insistence on hunting so often seemed rather immodest. On one occasion, instead of using the customary lances, she shot a third of the spoil with a crossbow Through the usual process of the courtiers telling the ambassadors and from the ambassadors it developing into an inviolable fact, Elizabeth had gained the reputation of being the greatest huntress in Europe. Her mother-in-law thought it rather brash. "As for me," she had once written to King James, "I can assure your Majesty that I shall die happy, when I have had the honour of seeing so worthy a princess as your daughter in this house, where she will receive all sorts of humble service, with affection so sincere." Now she wished that, for all the prestige Elizabeth had brought to the Palatinate, she could be dispatched home again.

But Elizabeth was there to stay, and it was Louisa Juliana who "retired to her dowry", as Elizabeth put it in 1614, "and well contented at her parting". By now Frederick had taken his mother's side. Elizabeth might indeed one day become Queen of England, there was no denying that she was the daughter of a king, but she was also, Frederick reasoned, his consort, and while she was in Germany that was how she ought to be treated. All this promoted a feeling of tension, which Elizabeth tried to ignore. She loved Frederick, despite his obvious boyishness, and although he might be brusque and might even refuse to discuss the subject of precedence with her, she did her best to take it all in her stride. When it was necessary, she asked Sir Henry Wotton to act as a go-between between her and her husband, confiding to Sir Henry that, despite Frederick's manner towards her in public, in private no-one could be more considerate or affectionate.

As late as 1617 the problem still rankled. "My Lord," she wrote then to one of her father's ambassadors,". . . The Prince of Anhalt understanding that I write to you hath desired me to clear him in a business which he hath been taxed with in England, that he should have been one of the chief causes of the dispute betwixt the Elector and me for place, which I assure you is false, for he did all the best offices he could to have it ended." By then however Elizabeth had her own ideas about how the problem should finally be resolved.

The problem of precedence was not the only thing which marred the early years of Elizabeth's married life. Her entourage behaved abominably. Elizabeth simply could not control them and consequently they treated her contemptuously. She even witnessed fights between them which she could do nothing to stop. The worst of these arose over a disagreement about some horses Lord Harington had exchanged with Elizabeth. Someone accused Harington of cheating. He hotly denied any such thing and Elizabeth refused to believe it. The quarrel soon developed into a brawl and, although the ageing Lord Harington was not one of the combatants, he decided that the time had come for him to return to England. He never completed the journey. At Worms he developed a fever and died. Elizabeth blamed herself and was stricken with remorse as well as grief.

Before she could even begin to adjust herself to life without the guidance of Lord Harington, the sixteen-year-old Princess was reminded that there were far too many English followers. Eager for sinecures and living at the Court's expense, they were unwilling to return to England. Schomberg tried to resolve her difficulties. He suggested that she should draw up a list of all those people who, she considered, should stay with her. Inevitably everyone petitioned to be on the list and Elizabeth, anxious not to offend anyone, achieved nothing at all.

Eventually the situation deteriorated so much that there had to be restrictions on Englishmen not officially attached to the Court entering the City. Those who were allowed to stay flagrantly flouted Germanic customs. A feud consequently developed and the Germans and the English had to sit at different tables.

Her servants treated Elizabeth with no more courtesy than they had treated the Germans. Moreover they were grasping. "But for me," the painstaking Schomberg wrote once, "Madame had been in debt more than £4,000—everybody robs her, even to the clothes and jewels she wears; and she gives, not of herself through liberality, but through importunities, complaints and tears."

"Be generally more strict," Schomberg pleaded with her, "liberty causes presumption; indifference in time spoils even the good . . . and all the suite of your highness, and of the prince too, believe that you dare not take offence, whatever they do."

By now her father had begun to press her about her generosity. How much had she given Anne Dudley, the impoverished niece of the Haringtons and a childhood friend from Coombe Abbey? Who else was profiting from being in her service?

"I received your letter," Elizabeth wrote to her father, "and understand that it is your Majesty's pleasure I should make known how Terrell that once served me came by the ruby buttons. I must tell you that at her going from me having served me painfully and very honestly ten years I was desirous some way to recompense her who had spent much and then never gotten anything so as these buttons being valued at the most but at £300 I freely gave them her for so much."

She continued to receive disapproving letters from her father. Although he had admitted to the Venetian ambassador on one occasion that, if he were to execute everyone who cheated the state, he would have no subjects left, King James would not tolerate anything that hinted even of generosity in his daughter's Court at Heidelberg. Elizabeth therefore spent many mornings carefully constructing letters to him to justify her position.

Her letters often included petitions on behalf of her servants and pleas to her father to influence them. Someone was having difficulty over a will, could he help with it? Schomberg was absent in Holland for a time, could King James persuade him to return?

Elizabeth's letters embraced an enormous range of subjects, but she never mentioned the "condition", which, much to her annoyance, her servants discussed openly. It was the general gibe at Court that she was the only person who knew nothing about it. But perhaps she felt there was no-one she could talk to. She was just seventeen, homesick and suddenly unwilling to grow up. To counteract her feeling of lethargy, she over-exerted herself: hunting, dancing, much to the concern of her mother-in-law, who had, despite every precaution, lost three children in infancy.

Throughout the autumn and winter Elizabeth continued tacitly to deny that she was pregnant. However, despite her protestations and Louisa Juliana's fears, a healthy child was born on 2 January 1614. Frederick proudly wrote to King James to tell him that he was now a "grandfather". The child was christened Frederick Henry.

King James wrote expressing wholehearted approval. The child might one day be King of England. In London most of the prisoners were liberated; a Bill was passed through Parliament announcing that the child was the "true and lawful successor to the crown after his mother the Princess Elizabeth"; King James sent a present of some pure gold drinking vessels for the baby and he promised an extra £2,000 a year for Elizabeth.

As soon as she could, Elizabeth put her son in the care of a nurse and resumed her normal activities. Life in the Heidelberg Court had become easier. Frederick's family had at last dispersed and Elizabeth could hunt and ride with impunity. For Louisa Juliana and Catherine, the erudite atmosphere of Heidelberg with its Calvinist University, had been replaced by the more bucolic pleasures of Kaiserslautern. When Elizabeth went to see them she derived a great deal of pleasure from feeding the cows, but on the whole she realised that their life was dull. There they lived, in a house which had no more claim to fame than the fact that it had been built by Barbarossa and overlooked the fishpond where, the legend ran, he had in 1230 attached a ring to one of the pike and the same fish had been caught alive in 1497.

Frederick's other sister, Charlotte, whom Elizabeth had found particularly bad-tempered, had married George William of Brandenburg. Her grandson, the first Prussian king, would one day marry a grand-daughter of Elizabeth. For the time being, however, Elizabeth put her out of her mind.

Her attention was focused on another marriage. This one would facilitate someone staying rather than going. Anne Dudley had, with some encouragement from Elizabeth, agreed to marry Count Schomberg, who had been in love with her for years. The marriage was a happy one, but it turned out sadly. Anne soon died in child-birth and a year afterwards Schomberg died too. Elizabeth reflected ruefully, as she would often do over the years, that friendship with her did not usually bring good fortune.

Characteristically, she did not reflect for long. There were too many journeys to be made up and down the Palatinate, too much correspondence to be attended to, and too many buildings to be admired. Like his father, and his Wittelsbach ancestors, Frederick was a fanatical builder. Palaces, turrets, ships, even statues of himself, complete with the garter insignia he had become so proud of and the symbolic Bavarian lion, were being constructed. Once he had a magnificent arch built in the garden overnight in honour of Elizabeth. His constant and expensive additions to the Castle were draining the resources of the Palatinate. He did not think about that.

Another child—Charles Louis—was born on 22 December 1617. His birth silenced the rumours that Frederick and Elizabeth had reverted to a platonic relationship. Eager to dispel those rumours, Elizabeth had taken waters on her doctor's advice. She had wanted the child, but his birth was marred by the news that both her parents were ill.

King James had not enhanced his reputation since Elizabeth had left for Germany. The corruption of the previous years had, almost inevitably, culminated in a series of scandals. His "little beagle", Robert Cecil, who, fortunately for him, was now dead, had been found to have been in the pay of Spain. Much worse for James, Robert Carr, on whom he had heaped every honour and all his trust, had betrayed him. The fairhaired young man had been implicated in a foul murder. The Overbury murder case had threatened the very foundations of the monarchy. But the King had won through at the cost merely of his good name and of his health.

Queen Anne who, for all her frivolity, had sustained at least a semblance of a moral standard in the Jacobean Court, was the more seriously ill of the two. Her gout had turned to a cruel form of dropsy and she could hardly move.

Elizabeth longed to go and see her parents, but again there was a precedence problem. Frederick insisted that if Elizabeth went to England he should come too. He must when he got there take precedence over Prince Charles.

This led to a long correspondence between ambassadors and, before the matter had been settled, Elizabeth discovered that she was pregnant again and could not make the journey. Frederick was relieved. He had suspected that King James would not be very welcoming.

By the time the child, a daughter, was born, King James had put all his other problems out of mind and was thinking only of his wife's will. He wanted her money and jewels and because Queen Anne was Danish he would only be entitled to them if they were willed to him. King James had never understood what went on in his wife's mind and now he found it completely incomprehensible. He could extract nothing from her. Anything might happen. Perhaps she would leave her money to the Catholic Church, to one of her servants, or to her son Charles. For the first time since their honeymoon King James was attentive, but it was of no avail. At the vital moment he was too ill to be with her and also too immersed in the company of his new favourite, George Villiers.

It was Prince Charles who was with her. "Your properties," he had asked just before she died, "am I to have those?"

"Yes," had been the answer. She had left nothing to her daughter or to the husband to whom she had been so loyal for so many years.

Her funeral was delayed because King James could not spare the money to pay for it. Beside her corpse, hour by hour, her ladies-in-waiting quarrelling among each other, kept a constant vigil.

"Sadness weighs my heart," wrote Elizabeth when she heard the news of her mother's death. It had been an unsatisfactory life and Elizabeth, thinking about it, determined that her marriage should never degenerate in the way her parents had done.

It was hardly likely to. Despite the difficulties Elizabeth's presence had caused, Frederick grew daily more entranced with her. His letters reveal something of what he felt. "My only dear heart," he would write when he was away. "Madame, your very true friend and very affectionate servant. . . . I beg you always to love me; and believe me that you are the only one I shall love until the grave, with all my affection." He would write in the soft, cultured, romantic language of France at least twice a week when he was away. He scrupulously observed even the most trivial anniversaries. Each letter was full of minutiae and gossip.

When he was at home, it seemed to Frederick that the Castle of Heidelberg itself had been revitalised by Elizabeth. It had recently been renovated and now boasted an Italian-Flemish frontage against its red brick. Its austere furniture, the hard upright chairs, the carpetless highly-polished floors, and the panelled and tapestried walls now somehow achieved an elegance which before might have been taken for severity. The numerous cabinets of pearwood and kingwood with pictures on the doors, the enamelled tables and enormous sideboards supported by figures of warriors and saints, could not fail to impress by their craftsmanship. A Hall of Mirrors was being built for Elizabeth which would add a modern note to a castle which had almost too many vividly coloured statues, carvings and paintings with bold brushwork and ancient themes. The whole Castle, now blended with a mixture of old and new from the fountain in the central courtyard with granite columns which had come from Charlemagne's Palace at Ingelheim, to Frederick's father's recent innovations on the west front. It was full of legends. A sybil foretelling the future had once lived in the turret. Sometimes even now there were reports that people had seen her casting a spell over the city. No less a relic than a finger of John the Baptist had found refuge there, the gift of Pope John two centuries earlier.

Frederick may have glanced up to the library window where Elizabeth so often studied new languages and, between reading light romantic novels, examined the books in the Heidelberg collection. The original of Luther's translation of the Book of Isaiah was among them, as well as old manuscripts of Thucydides and Plutarch.

Frederick longed to spend more time with her. He envied the time other people spent with her such as the clever Wotton who thought that "an ambassador [was] an honest man sent to lie abroad for the good of his country". Frederick was not jealous, but despondent. He blamed himself partly for the precedence problem, which weighed on him as heavily as it did Elizabeth. If only he had stood up against King James.

He longed to please her and so he concentrated on contriving a beautiful walk with a garden to remind her of the one at Coombe Abbey. Stretching down from the Castle on the rocky hillside he had trees planted, flowers exotic and wild and fragrant, of a hundred different scents so that every time she walked in the garden and looked far below at the river Neckar or sat by the fountain listening to the mechanically devised music which must have seemed to have issued from the little streams that meandered among the grass, or from the shrubberies, she could remember all the things she had enjoyed most in her childhood and create in her mind a vision of paradise which she would always yearn to return to. For the truth was that as the wooded hills around Heidelberg changed again and again from the white of the cherry blossom in the spring, to red and gold in autumn and the bleak desolation of winter, Elizabeth and Frederick were as happy as they would ever be.

CHAPTER SIX

Frederick at first did try to dispel his feelings of gloomy premonition and melancholy. He made an effort to find pleasure in simple things: the monkeys that romped around Elizabeth's bed in the mornings; the hunting parties; and the pleasure excursions. He tried to convince himself that, as he looked above the garden at the Castle, which overlooked the Neckar and the vineyards of the Palatinate which stretched layer upon layer far into the distance, the air of security and serenity it conveyed as it glowed in the sunlight was not deceptive.

But even if the Castle itself was secure, the truth was that it did not symbolise the Palatinate of which it was the apex. Far away near Regensburg were the Upper Palatinate lands, which were disorientated from Heidelberg, geographically and religiously. They were vulnerable and completely indefensible and often quite forgotten by Frederick. It was Heidelberg that he loved and his mind somehow could not encompass those diffuse Upper Palatinate lands as well.

Elizabeth had first become aware of the problems which confronted Frederick in August 1614, when, after listening to a long sermon aimed at improving his moral welfare, he had taken over the administration of the Palatinate. This was as far as his ambitions led him. But for his advisers and friends it did not seem to be enough. Maurice in particular was planning another future for his nephew. Surely Elizabeth and Frederick so well-matched, so well-connected, and so popular, must play a more prominent part in history than visiting outposts of the Palatinate, building new palaces like the one already begun at Franckenthal and performing the routines of ceremony and administration.

It was unlikely that anything radical could be done on the home front, it was foreign affairs which occupied their minds. Unfortunately for Frederick, his family had a tradition of belligerency. Under Elector Frederick III, the Palatinate had supported the Huguenots and the Netherlands revolt. Frederick's father had been a staunch Calvinist, leader of the Protestants in Germany and a strong opponent of the Hapsburgs. Now Frederick himself as Elector Palatine was the natural leader of the Protestants in Germany. As such, if he were strong (and perhaps foolhardy) enough, he could challenge the might of the Hapsburgs. Frederick however was not strong and it seems that his advisers, Christian of Anhalt, the Duc de Bouillon, and even Count Schomberg, were not astute enough to appreciate this. For all his titles, Frederick was not the man to lead the Protestants against the Catholics in Germany. When he realised the implications of his position he became morose, depressed and subject to psychosomatic illnesses.

Religious unrest had been festering in Germany for over fifty years. Charles V had been too pre-occupied by his wars with France to want to rock the religious boat and in 1555 his Treaty of Ausburg with the Electors had laid it down that within the States of the Empire, the religion of the subject should be the religion of his prince. A year later he had abdicated and his vast possessions were split up between his son, Philip II of Spain and his nephew Maximilian II who became Holy Roman Emperor. Since the main concern of the Austrian Hapsburgs was to keep out the Turks, even had they wanted to, and not all of them did, at first they were in no position to upset the Treaty of Ausburg or to restore Roman Catholicism.

This was left to Philip II in his unsuccessful attempts to invade England and put down the revolt in the Netherlands. He also carried on the family feud with the French Valois kings and France was where Protestant and Catholic really came to blows. From 1562 to 1598 the country was devastated by the bloody Wars of Religion. These gave the more warlike Germans the chance to work off their fanaticism away from home by intervening on one side or the other.

Philip died in 1598 and his son Philip III turned out to be a very different character. In 1604 he signed a peace treaty with the equally pacific James I; in 1609 he concluded a twelve-year truce with the Dutch, and in 1611 he married his daughter, Anne of Austria, to the youthful Louis XIII of France. Meanwhile the suppression by the Emperor of Protestantism in Donaüwörth in 1608 and the expulsion of Protestants by several Roman Catholic bishops in southern Germany had indicated that the Austrian Hapsburgs no longer intended to be on the defensive. The situation might have been resolved had not the constitutional machinery of the Empire virtually broken down. The more moderate Lutherans, too, might have reached some sort of agreement with the Catholics but for the fear that they would have to disgorge the Church lands which they had seized. But at bottom, the spread of Calvinism and the Counter-Reformation made the representatives on each side unwavering fanatics. "What a fine God you are!" Frederick's father had once declared while he tore the Host in pieces to demonstrate his disbelief in transubstantiation, "You think you are stronger than I; we shall see." Shortly after this the leader of the Catholics, Ferdinand of Styria, announced that he would sooner lose everything than tolerate a heretic. It was obvious that neither side would compromise.

"The world," Sir Walter Raleigh had written, thinking of his old enemy Spain with the vast resources of her Empire and the increasing stupidity of her rulers; and of Austria, uneasy and anxious to preserve the status quo; and of Germany, resurgent, singleminded and overconfident. "The world," he had continued sadly "is in a slumber and this long calm will shortly break out into some terrible tempest." In 1618 a comet flashed across the sky, presaging, so everyone said, catastrophe.

It was to come sooner than people expected. As so often happens in the case of an unpleasant inevitability everyone was preoccupied with something else. In England a vociferous opposition party was forming while King James ogled his latest favourite, the handsome and extravagant George Villiers. The Hapsburg Empire was threatened while the Emperor devoted himself to his beautiful wife. Frederick, the hope of the Protestant cause, thought of Elizabeth's garden and pulled down the fortifications of Heidelberg Castle to assist his building programme. By now Heidelberg was a focus for intrigue and that intrigue centred on Frederick and the throne of Bohemia.

Bohemia held a position all of its own in the Empire. In the first place it was the only kingdom in all that agglomeration of principalities and lesser states. For centuries the Kings of Bohemia had played a leading role in Central Europe. Long before the Hapsburgs had worked their way to the crown, that crown had been made elective and the power of election lay with the three Estates of the realm. As the King of Bohemia played a decisive part in electing the Holy Roman Emperor, it had always been a corner-stone of Hapsburg policy to make sure of the Bohemian crown, in order to retain their hold on the Imperial title.

It was even more vital now, and not just for the Austrian Hapsburgs. The command of the sea was firmly in Dutch and English hands. The Spanish Netherlands would be cut off unless the Spanish Hapsburgs could keep up their communications from their Italian possessions northward through Imperial territory. If a Protestant were ever elected King of Bohemia, that could mean a Protestant or non-Hapsburg emperor. The consequences for Spain didn't bear thinking about.

What made it worse was that the people of Bohemia were fiercely independent and totally unpredictable. Nine-tenths of them were Protestants into the bargain. Jan Hus had gone to the stake in 1415, but his teachings lived on. When the Reformation came, a minority of Hussites, while remaining independent tended to favour the Catholic side, while the majority supported the Lutherans. Some even became Lutherans themselves. The Hapsburgs' hopes were pinned on these divisions.

Recent Bohemian history had been no less eventful than usual. In 1605 the Hapsburg family, realising that the childless Emperor

Rudolph, for all his astheticism, was administratively incompetent, handed over the governing of the Empire to his brother Matthias. Rudolph, retained the title of Emperor and was put in charge of Bohemia. There he practised alchemy and kept a pet lion.

By 1609, Rudolph, by nature an appeaser, had granted the Bohemians greater independence and religious toleration in the Letter of Majesty. Frederick's scheming and staunchly Protestant father openly supported this move.

By 1617 Rudolph had died but his Letter of Majesty was still the pride of every Czech. Then the Emperor Matthias announced that his successor would be none other than Ferdinand of Styria and also nominated him for the vacant throne of Bohemia. Predominantly Protestant Bohemia knew about Ferdinand's reputation, but they let themselves be persuaded by his suave assurances that he would observe the Letter of Majesty.

Brought up from the cradle to believe that where the Catholic cause was concerned, the end always justified the means, Ferdinand had no intention of abiding by his promises. As soon as he was elected he curbed the Bohemians' cherished liberties. The ensuing disquiet culminated in the famous defenestration of Prague when two Catholic deputies and their secretary were thrown from a window. Miraculously none of them was killed, but, as the Bohemians' leader, Count Thurn, told the Czechs, it was either revolt or defeat. They chose revolt. They would rule Bohemia as they wanted.

A provisonal government was formed representing the three Estates of Bohemia. Wenceslaus of Ruppa was chosen as President and Count Thurn, a foreigner who had difficulty in speaking the Czech language, took over the army. The Jesuits, who were generally used as scapegoats for the Bohemians' troubles, were expelled.

Matthias and Ferdinand sent an army to restore their influence and Charles Emmanuel, Duke of Savoy, rustled up a counter army under Mansfeld, the foremost soldier in Germany. Mansfeld's Protestant army besieged and took the Czech town of Pilsen, which still had Catholic sympathies, and he secured a temporary peace.

In March 1619 Matthias died and in all the petty courts of the Empire began a vast network of intrigue over who should be Emperor. Henry Wotton wrote to England: "the main question is whether a new Emperor will be made by the sword or by election."

The German Protestants had chosen to defeat Ferdinand through constitutional means and they began to consider other possible candidates for the imperial throne. Frederick himself approached the ascetic and cautious Maximilian of Bavaria who refused sardonically adding, as Sir Henry Wotton put it in a dispatch to King James, "how sensible he was of the honour . . . he might invite your Majesty's most virtuous daughter (who hath filled these countries with her excellent fame) to come and take possession in Bavaria of her woods and fields and to kill all there that hath either wings or feet." In fact no suitable alternative was found and all the Protestant plots and much-debated manoevres came to nothing. At the crucial moment John George of Saxony, who, as usual, was drunk when he most needed to be clear-headed, had an argument. In a huff he voted for Ferdinand and even Frederick, not wanting to be the only dissident, voted for Ferdinand as well. Ferdinand was therefore unanimously voted Emperor of the Holy Roman Empire.

Stretching from Poland to the Ottoman Empire, to Savoy, to Lorraine and to Hamburg, the Holy Roman Empire incorporated a multitude of races with different cultures and languages. It needed a man of infinite tact and ability to hold it together and maintain peace.

When Elizabeth heard the result of the election, she was furious. She wrote scathingly to Sir Dudley Carleton in England "they have chosen here a blind Emperor, for he hath but one eye, and that not very good. I am afraid he will be lousy, for he hath not money to buy himself clothes."

Three days after the election the Bohemians disowned Ferdinand as their king and began looking for someone to replace him. The first person they approached was John George of Saxony, but he wisely refused. They then turned to Frederick who, they argued, being young would "better accommodate himself to the customs of the kingdom." It was what everyone had been expecting.

Poor Frederick, who had been canvassing for his election for some months, now drew back. It was obvious that it would be a dangerous venture. The Bohemian army had already marched under Count Thurn as far as Vienna, provoking a direct conflict with the Emperor. They had been chased back to the borders of Bohemia by the Imperialists, who had only been halted by the timely invasion of Austria by the Transylvanian, Bethlen Gabor. They were unlikely to be so fortunate in the future.

Frederick could not reach a decision. The problem totally absorbed him. On the one hand was his mother beseeching him not to be so foolish, not to jeopardise his inheritance for something so unstable, not to challenge the might of Austria. The Princes of Saxony and Bavaria also warned him. The Elector of Cologne observed that Spain and Austria would never relinquish Bohemia whatever else they might do and that, if Frederick accepted the crown, a twenty, thirty, or forty year war would ensue. Even the Duc de Bouillon, while supporting any military assistance Frederick might give to the Bohemians, did not encourage him to accept such a perilous throne. And Lord Doncaster cautioned him to "take into contemplation as well the number and qualities of his enemies, as the affection and power of his friends."

Frederick did his best. He knew that Spain was as opposed to Protestantism as Austria was, but he hoped that the traditional hostility between France and Spain might, if necessary, bring France to his side. He also believed that England would support him. Nevertheless he was uneasy. He had an instinctive feeling that it was wrong.

But on the other side was Elizabeth, young, beautiful, idealistic, with an imperishable zeal shining in her eyes, remembering Henry, urging and importuning Frederick to act as her brother would have done: to become the benefactor of the Protestant cause. She wrote fervently to him, "since you are persuaded that the throne to which you are invited is a vocation from God, by whose Providence are all things ordained and directed, then assuredly you ought not to shrink from the duty imposed; nor, if such be your persuasion, shall I repine whatever consequences may ensue, not even though I should be forced to part from my last jewel, and to suffer actual hardship, shall I ever repent the election." How she asked, could he have had the audacity to marry a king's daughter if he did not know how to take the opportunity of becoming a king himself? Had not the Hapsburg Empress invited her to Ratisbon with the intention, she had only discovered just in time, of murdering her? She reminded Frederick about the question of precedence. Only recently when King James's ambassador and former favourite, Lord Doncaster, had arrived in Heidelberg to find that Frederick was in Heilbrunn had that problem been emphasised again. To avoid being received by Elizabeth before Frederick's return, knowing that such an action would be interpreted as recognition of her superiority, Doncaster and his entourage, which included John Donne as Chaplain, had stayed in the town. Elizabeth however, had forbidden the markets to sell food to his agents. In the end Doncaster had had to come to the Castle and once there Elizabeth tactfully, for she was growing used to such episodes, had avoided seeing him until Frederick returned. It was an example of how irksome the whole issue could be and she pressed her point home to Frederick. If he took the Bohemian throne, the problem would be resolved.

It was also the sort of situation for which Frederick's dedicated, if somewhat opportunist adviser, Christian of Anhalt, had been scheming for years and Frederick had never gone against his advice. And then there was Prince Maurice asking Louisa Juliana if there was any green baize in Heidelberg. "Certainly," she had answered, "what do you want it for?" "To make a fool's cap for him who might be a king and will not." had been the reply. Even the Doge of Venice seemed favourably inclined towards his candidature.

A treaty of allegiance existed between Frederick and the Duke of Savoy; the Landgrave of Hesse promised to stand by him, and wasn't Frederick connected to nearly all the Protestant princes in Europe? Surely they would support him. Elizabeth, who was fascinated by pedigrees, ennumerated them. The list was formidable: Maurice of

Nassau, King Christian of Denmark, Gustavus Adolphus of Sweden, George William of Brandenburg and of course King James of England. A religious fanatic in Heidelberg began preaching the Bohemian cause.

"Alas," said Frederick, "if I accept the crown, I shall be accused of ambition—if I reject it, I shall be branded with cowardice. However I may decide, there is no peace for me or my country."

"I have seen nothing of Bohemia this week," he wrote weakly to Elizabeth in August. How he hoped he would never see anything of the Czechs again. "It seems it is the place where Ferdinand acquired a crown; he could well have lost two of them. God bless him. He is a very happy prince for he has the good fortune to be hated by everyone." The nagging uncertainty continued. Something held him back. There was only one faint glimmer of hope. He suspected that his father-in-law would disapprove and so he decided to ask his opinion.

Elizabeth was reluctant to do this. Wasn't her father the arch-protector of the status quo? Besides, immersed in the domestic bliss of the Buckingham family, King James found it impossible to understand how his children in Heidelberg could not be equally contented. Didn't he send them enormous quantities of English beer every quarter? Weren't the children enough to satisfy his daughter? But Elizabeth was eager for new adventures. Long ago she had started on another journey dressed in a brown taffeta dress, which had seemed sumptuous at the beginning of the journey but when she reached England it hardly compared with the finery of the people surrounding her. Journeys tended to lead to better things.

It was therefore reluctantly that she wrote to the Marquis of Buckingham on 1 September 1619. But before her letter reached the favourite, let alone the King, the irrecoverable decision had been taken.

The Czechs began to feign misgivings. Perhaps they might not give Frederick the crown after all. They dangled it before the dreaming young man whose wife, it was said, told him she would rather eat sauerkraut with a king than roast beef with an elector. Had he ever refused her anything? Could he refuse her what she professed she most longed for now, particularly when she was pregnant with another child? He thought of all those engagements he had attended alone, he relived all her taunts a hundred times over. He determined to make himself worthy of her, to equal his irreproachable rival, Prince Henry. And so he accepted.

The Duke of Zweibrucken, his brother-in-law, took over his responsibilities in the Palatinate. His mother left her peaceful retirement to look after the two younger children. "Alas, alas," she predicted, "the Palatinate is lost in Bohemia."

CHAPTER SEVEN

They began their journey at 8 o'clock on the morning of 7 October 1619, accompanied by 153 baggage wagons. In effect they slunk out of Heidelberg, avoiding the main street, heading towards the East. Frederick Henry came with them. Elizabeth's first child, whom the Heidelbergers loved so much, like his mother, would never see the Castle or the gardens again. But among the Palatine family, seated in their coaches, watching the Neckar and the red façade of the Castle receding into the distance, there was an unmistakable feeling of optimism. It was rather like setting out on a crusade. Frederick, to lend credit to the expedition, had given up his precious pack of hounds as a gesture of his devotion to the Protestant cause and his relinquishment of worldly pleasures. If he had sought self-abnegation the journey to Prague would have been enough for even the most hardened stoic.

Outside courts like that of Heidelberg and the wealthy trading cities the rest of Germany was not only feudal, but backward, even by seventeenth century standards. Not only were the nobles and peasants alike dedicated to drinking one another under the table, but they also lacked almost any ethnic culture of their own—the little they did have being derived from France, Spain and Italy and normally displayed merely for the sake of foreign ambassadors. Even their literature was debased in dull theological polemic.

This Elizabeth must have discerned as she travelled through the other petty courts of Germany. But on the road to Amberg a large stone, dislodged by the wheel of her coach, hit her full in the face with such a strong impact that she fainted and for the next part of her journey she lay down only half aware of the erratic movement of the coach and not at all aware of any form of art. She insisted that the journey should not be interrupted on her account. There were, she knew, compensations in lying down. The view outside had been a depressing one. At the edge of the road the bodies of hanged thieves could be seen as they might have been over a thousand years beforehand. Everything throughout the journey had revealed that Germany was in a state of abject poverty. Peasants, whose average lifespan was only 22, had lined the streets. But whereas on her wedding journey, Elizabeth had seen the population looking their best, wearing costumes it may have taken them a year to sew, there were now starving people, racked with disease, living in damp little shacks, which they often shared with their livestock. It was the same throughout Germany. Misery, disease and ignorance. A country riddled with superstition. Alchemy and black magic, frequently practised by princes, terrified the peasant population. Elizabeth and Frederick, convinced by Frederick's preacher, Andreas Scultetus, that they were taking on the second city of Babylon as part of their divine mission, travelled accompanied by their Flanders' tapestries, their damask table-cloths and their rare porcelain.

As they journeyed on, the soldiers of the Palatinate followed them and Count Fürstenberg, imperial envoy, also pursued them, begging Frederick to pause and resolve their differences through negotiation rather than leading everyone into conflict. But Frederick had given his promise and he would not retract. The decision had already been made. In taking on Prague, they were saving the Christian world.

Resolutely the party drove on to Waldsassen on the border of Bohemia, where Frederick had arranged to meet the Czech envoys. The delegation of Czechs convinced him that he would be welcome in Bohemia. Frederick's young brother, Count Louis Palatine, and his adviser Christian of Anhalt were also there shivering in the cold waiting to greet them. Elizabeth remembered Waldsassen afterwards because it was there that she was first officially addressed as a queen. The speech of welcome, made by Baron Ruppa, referred to the general assumption that Elizabeth had played a vital role in influencing her husband to accept the crown. "Sir," Elizabeth responded, "what I have done for the honour of God and the good of our religion has been done with hearty goodwill, and in future my favour and affection shall never be wanting."

From Waldsassen they passed through the wild landscape of Bohemia and on to Prague.

The City of Prague was a source of pride to the Czechs. With its gables and towers and dormer windows, its pine forests and sloping terraces, syringa trees and yew hedges, cherry trees, its arcades, its belfries, and basilicas, everything proclaimed it to be prosperous and fertile. And the enormous ornate Powder Gate, Charles' bridge, founded by Charles IV in 1357, the bleak and foreboding Hradčany Castle, where Elizabeth and Frederick were to live, the Schwartzenberg Palace, the Jewish cemetery dating from the thirteenth century, the Pinkas synagogue. It was the seat of the first University in Central Europe and it had the first botanical garden. The rich collection, which had been amassed under Rudolph of paintings and antiquities, the Cathedral of St Vitus, all pointed to the national characteristics of the Czechs; piety, patronage, tolerance, nobility, loyalty to tradition.

However, despite their knowledge of the past, the Czechs seemed to be only dimly aware that a geographical position such as theirs in the heartland of central Europe necessitated a good defence policy. To them learning about the past was more important than dreary practicalities to safeguard the future. By 1619 such beliefs had sapped the genius of the Czechs. Prague was no longer at the height of her golden age. The time had passed when Kepler and Tycho Brahe had practised there as Imperial astronomers and Dürer had painted his mystical paintings. The clocks which had fascinated the Emperor Rudolph had stopped ticking; the water machines for the gardens no longer functioned, and most of the stables were empty. Instead the students of the university discussed the crisis.

But on the day when Elizabeth and Frederick entered Prague—21 October 1619—even that was forgotten. The whole city, Czechs, Italians and Jews, came out to greet the young man they supposed to be the second Ziska.

"We arrived here," Elizabeth wrote the next day, "being received with great show of love of all sorts of people." The bells pealed and guns were fired.

Frederick, looking magnificent in brown and silver, rode on a charger, Elizabeth entered alone in a coach with a cover of violet and gold. Behind her in another were her ladies and behind them, accompanied by his attendants, was Frederick Henry.

Glancing out of the window of her coach, Elizabeth could see that the crowds were less constrained than those in Heidelberg. The people coming to greet them were strangely dressed and playing wild music. It was almost, she felt, barbaric—shouting, crying, gesticulating. She was partly embarrassed and partly amused. As they addressed Frederick and began dancing and banging wooden cups together, she broke into a burst of laughter. Frederick managed to appear courteous and grave. When Elizabeth had composed herself she begged him to let them know "how much she regretted being ignorant of their language, which she would forthwith set about learning."

They then went to offer thanks in the Cathedral of St Vitus. Here it was Frederick's turn to be surprised. There were so many effigies of saints and holy relics that it could have been a Catholic church. They must, he pronounced at once, be destroyed. The Czechs decided not to let that mar his welcome. He would change his mind, they felt. The festivities continued.

As Elizabeth and Frederick were led into the Hradčany Castle, the women lay down in the street and kissed the hem surrounding the hoop of Elizabeth's dress. The men whispered among themselves that with Frederick's great wealth anything could be achieved and the 50,000 guilden, which had been spent on the reception, would be nothing compared to their gain.

On 3 November 1619 Frederick was crowned in the Cathedral of St Vitus. The procession to that altar was headed by the hereditary office holders with the chief server symbolically carrying two loaves of bread, one covered with gold and the other with silver. Then came the cupbearers with two vessels of wine, again with one covered in gold and the other in silver. He was followed by the chief office-holders of the kingdom: the Chief Secretary carrying the sceptre, the Chief Judge a gold apple, the Chief Citizen, the crown, the Chief Chamberlain the mitre and the Chief Marshal the sword. At the end of the procession came Frederick with the Administrator on his right and the Elder on his left.

During the service the people came forward to touch the crown as a gesture of homage and afterwards the fountain in the main square ran wine for more than an hour. Thousands of coins endorsed with the words: "God and the Estates gave me the Crown" were distributed among the people.

When Elizabeth was crowned three days later during a shorter ceremony, because of her advanced pregnancy, she arranged for bread to be distributed rather than coins. During her coronation she was reminded of the "changefulness of kingdoms and empires, whereby all kings and queens of this world are admonished to aspire from these fleeting and frail possessions to those that are eternal and immoveable." Much more welcome to Elizabeth were the words *Vivat Elizabetha, Amen, Amen*, which greeted her as she left the Church. Now at last she had lived up to the expectations of the English people, and her own expectations, and gone, at last, was the problem of precedence.

The people of England were delighted about Frederick and Elizabeth's elevation. King James, however, was not. He forbade his subjects to pray for the King of Bohemia because, he insisted, Frederick was nothing more than the Elector Palatine. Unwittingly Frederick and Elizabeth had come up against the most fervent of King James' beliefs, his staunch acceptance of the Divine Right of Kings. Nothing could alter that. Under his code no people could remove a king, however unjust they might believe him to be. Kings were answerable only to God. Frederick, as a Calvinist, felt otherwise. He believed that if it was justified, a king could be removed. Moreover King James felt that for practical reasons Frederick's decision was wrong. How could Frederick repel the might of Austria? The Roman Catholic Emperor would never accept a Protestant majority in the Electoral College. Moreover

King James was offended. Why had they not waited for his advice? He liked to be consulted. When he learnt that Frederick and Elizabeth had accepted the Bohemian crown, he told their envoy, Baron Dhona, that he "would not embark [his subjects] in an unjust and needless quarrel."

However, he would, he promised, protect the Palatinate, since that was rightfully Frederick's and he did not want to be accused of depriving his grandchildren of their lawful inheritance. He found the whole matter tiresome and, worse still, ominous. "A rash step," the Spanish Ambassador in Vienna had described it as and it would be an understatement to say that King James was inclined to agree with him. Hoping somehow to keep the peace he sent Lord Doncaster on a wild goose chase round Europe to try and convince Ferdinand that the Bohemians were now in a strong position. In the meantime he fretted and fumed in Whitehall.

In Prague it was very different. There Elizabeth and Frederick were thoroughly enjoying themselves under the blissful impression, which had been encouraged by various diplomats, that King James would come round to their way of thinking eventually. The hounds had been recalled and the disapproval of Louisa Juliana and the failure of the Elector of Saxony to congratulate Frederick were all forgotten in the endless pursuit of happiness.

But being a queen wasn't all that Elizabeth had anticipated. She did not like the Czechs. The servants upset wine over her when they poured it out and sullenly they refused to learn a foreign language. Gaucheness always irritated Elizabeth and, because she did not anticipate making any new friends in Prague, she did not make a great effort either to learn Czech or to improve her German. For companionship she relied on the people who had come with her, particularly the young, robust, beautiful, proud Amalia de Solms who had, to some extent, taken Anne Dudley's place. Like Elizabeth she was blissfully unaware of her precarious position in Prague.

Frederick did nothing to upset their false illusions. He hoped that by securing alliances with the Protestant Princes he would guarantee the safety of his kingdom. Already Bethlen Gabor and the Bohemian Count Thurn were marching on Vienna. With support Frederick might in one swift campaign defeat the Hapsburgs. On the other hand he might not. The Protestant Princes who met Frederick at Amberg cast a glance at the preoccupied Hapsburgs in Vienna and decided that for the time being they could afford to give Frederick promises of assistance. He would only learn too late how fallacious these promises were. To the Princes of Germany no cause mattered so much as the protection of their own territories.

Frederick then turned his attention to Turkey and the Sultan, whose power was generally regarded in Christendom as having been engendered by the devil. Nevertheless Frederick wanted him as an ally. The Sultan, however, was not the sort of friend the Czechs wanted. Already they had noticed that Frederick's views on many things were at marked variance with their own.

There were the teachings of Frederick's preacher, Scultetus, who had harangued the people over their holy statues and had told them that the King and Queen would not pass over a certain bridge until the crucifix on it had been destroyed. As this crucifix had miraculously survived two centuries of battles and political up-heavals, the Czechs were unanimously outraged. They were begin-ning to doubt Frederick's religious sincerity. How could he seriously consider the Sultan as an ally? Already Frederick was beginning to experience some of the difficulties of being a monarch: the obstinacy of public opinion and worse still, unlike his father-in-law, the knowledge that his powers were severely limited. Even on internal affairs he was restricted. When, on the advice of his counsellor, Camerarius, he tried to sort out some of the financial problems of the country, which was prospering agriculturally and commercially, but unable to pay her soldiers, he was met with sullen resentment. Hadn't Frederick all the resources of the Palatinate at his disposal? Couldn't he make do with them?

Wherever he turned there were problems to be resolved and criticism to refute. In Prague Elizabeth had laughed with her page when he derisively decorated his hat with one of the circular loaves the peasant women were presenting to their queen on her saint's day. Simultaneously the tide of public opinion began to turn against her. There were disparaging comments on the low cut of her dresses. There was disappointment at what the Czechs saw as the profligacy of the new Court. They were shocked when they saw Frederick swimming naked in the river in front of Elizabeth's ladies-in-waiting. They did not approve of the uninvited guests who turned up in such large numbers at Prague expecting to be housed and fed. "The foreigner" they now called Elizabeth. The only commendable thing about her as far as the Czechs were concerned at this time was that for the first time in the last one hundred years a royal child was to be born in Prague.

The child who was born at such a useful moment on 17 December 1619, was christened Prince Rupert. The ladies of Prague, abiding by an ancient custom, insisted on being present at the birth. They had hoped, also in respect of past tradition, that the child would have a Czech name. The fact that he didn't did not diminish his welcome. The pageantry marking the christening some time later was as sumptuous as that which had marked his parents' coronation. A huge temporary palace was constructed and a tilting match was contested. The elders bestowed on him the title of the Duke of Lithuania and people carried marvellous presents for him to the Castle. There were cheering parades as the guests came for the christening and the beautiful Turkish horse the child's half-barbaric godfather, Bethlen Gabor, had sent him was watched with such admiration and astonishment by the Czechs that they almost forgot that Gabor was the ally of the Turks, who were intent on pillaging the Christian world.

In fact on various occasions the Czechs did show that they had a remarkable capacity for putting things out of their minds. They continued even now to do everything they could to please Elizabeth and Frederick. They hinted that one day they might be Emperor and Empress and in the meantime they agreed to make the throne hereditary and recognise Frederick Henry as heir after his father. Some of them wished that Rupert could take precedence over his brothers, but Frederick, quite naturally, insisted that his heir must be Frederick Henry.

How he wished that Elizabeth's beauty and charm would work the same magic they had on the Heidelbergers on the strange

F71

eastern people he now ruled. There was an elusive quality about Elizabeth which could never be entirely recaptured in paint or verse. It was almost wasted in Prague. The coronation pictures had been very unsatisfactory and even the painter Honthorst's efforts to capture completely the determination and animation of her oval face, her proud features, her darkening hair, were not completely successful. The ageing, but doting, Sir Henry Wotton compared her beauty with that of the stars, the birds and the flowers:

> *You meaner beauties of the night,*
> *That poorly satisfy our eyes*
> *More by your number than your light,*
> *You common people of the skies;*
> *What are you, when the Moon shall rise?*
>
> *You curious chanters of the wood,*
> *That warble forth Dame Nature's lays,*
> *Thinking your passions understood*
> *By your weak accents;*
> *What's your praise when Philomel her voice shall raise?*
>
> *You violets that first appear,*
> *By your pure purple mantle known;*
> *Like the proud virgins of the year,*
> *As if the Spring were all your own;*
> *What are you, when the rose is blown?*
>
> *So when my mistress shall be seen,*
> *In form and beauty of her mind;*
> *By virtue first, then choice, a queen,*
> *Tell me, if she were not designed*
> *Th' eclipse and glory of her kind?*

As Sir Henry Wotton was compiling that poem in London, Elizabeth was arranging masques and hunting parties on the White Mountain overlooking Prague. There were endless visitors to see the new King and Queen. Louisa Juliana came with her daughter, Catherine, whom she was hoping to marry to the Duke of Saxe-

Weimar. Nothing, however, came of that. With each new batch of guests came more parties and more festivities.

From the Court it hardly seemed that the fighting season had begun again. There was no atmosphere of despondency among the Queen's entourage or any whisper of the fact that the Bohemians had lost the skirmishes in Lower Austria and that, divided by the rift between Count Thurn and Christian of Anhalt, the Czech troops were slowly retreating to the frontier. Throughout the winter there had hardly been a mention of Mansfeld's troops, sent by the Protestant Duke of Savoy, which were starving at the Catholic stronghold they had taken at Pilsen. But all the time the diplomats had been busy trying to isolate Prague and confine the imminent conflict. Ferdinand could wait no longer to reclaim his kingdom. By March he had outlawed Frederick and by the end of April he had issued an ultimatum against him. By July the Princes of the Union and the Catholic League were signing the Treaty of Ulm, which sought to maintain the status quo outside Bohemia. Maximilian of Bavaria, brother-in-law of the Emperor, was supporting him goaded on by the promise of the Palatinate and its electoral dignity, be sending 25,000 troops under the proficient, if reputedly ruthless general, Tilly. The Pope was levying a tithe on all Church land in Italy to raise money for Ferdinand. The King of Poland agreed to the recruiting of Cossacks from his territories to support the Imperialists. The Lutheran John George of Saxony, who regarded Calvinism as a challenge to the fabric of law and order was for the moment neutral. Spain was inevitably on Ferdinand's side. King Louis of France, who Frederick had believed would support him, concentrated on neutralising the combatants. Even Bethlen Gabor for a time was wooed into a temporary peace, and Maurice of Nassau, with such a strong opposition, felt he could do nothing more than grant Frederick 50,000 florins a month and a few troops. No more was mentioned of pieces of baize.

The Margrave of Bradenburg found that domestic problems precluded him from involving himself in his brother-in-law's problems. James I, ailing now and lacking astute advisers, and preoccupied with the idea of a possible marriage between his son

Charles and the Infanta of Spain, pandered to Ferdinand and effectually became his puppet. Sweden was preoccupied with a war in Poland. So all Elizabeth and Frederick's connections, their lineal descent from twenty-five emperors and thirty kings, which had been vaunted at their marriage, counted for nothing.

It was not long before the Upper Palatinate had been invaded by over 20,000 Spanish troops. Producing large revenues for Frederick, it was Ferdinand's way of besieging Bohemia. A lampoonist ominously portrayed Spinola, the Spanish general, as writing to Frederick in biblical terms: "Behold, I send my servants before thy face, who shall prepare the way for the King of Spain through Germany into Bohemia."

Louisa Juliana had just enough time to write to King James telling him that the Spanish army "is already at our door" and begging him to help his children before she fled to Berlin with Charles Louis and the young Elizabeth. But still King James would not lend his wholehearted support. The Spanish Ambassador, Gondomar was much nearer to him than the composers of those frantic letters which could so easily be put aside, hardly read and wholly forgotten. King James had soon been thoroughly hoodwinked into believing that when Frederick gave up Prague, the Spanish would meekly retire from the Palatinate. It was a very convenient thing to believe. It gave the old King time.

He decided not to send an army, although he did not obstruct the small army of volunteers led by Sir Horace Vere which was setting out to the Palatinate from England. Nor did he stop Prince Charles sending his savings to help his sister.

In the meantime Frederick felt lost and trapped. "A foul labyrinth in which he will certainly lose himself," Pope Paul V had described the acceptance of the throne of Bohemia. Now cartoons, probably emanating from Vienna, were portraying Frederick as a lion trampled under the wheel of fortune, with Ferdinand the eagle, triumphant above.

Frederick did everything he could somehow to redeem the worsening situation. However he was not equipped to be a great soldier or statesman. He had never even been instructed in military affairs and his despondency was so obvious that it was in vain that he tried to rally the disease-ridden and disorderly troops, a large proportion of whom he was supporting with his private money. It was hopeless to appeal to the Czech nobility for funds when they saw the style in which Elizabeth lived. Besides the Czechs were disillusioned with their Calvinist King, enraged by the preachings of Scultetus and out of tune with the romance which Elizabeth and Frederick enacted throughout their everyday lives. The continual stream of presents, the perpetual whispered words of devotion were beginning to jar. Only a few people could wholeheartedly join in the hymn written at the end of 1620:

"Our king and sovereign Frederick the Second deign to protect, O Lord: and do protect all his lands, deign also to bless Her Grace the Queen, and to their whole house give growth and prosperity."

Already, as that was being written, people were arranging for their families to leave Bohemia. The seven-year-old Frederick Henry was secretly sent to Holland with his uncle, Louis Palatine. They travelled in a plain coach which was filled with Elizabeth's jewels and valuables.

It was generally known that Maximilian's troops, in principle not much better than Frederick's, but unlike his adequately clothed and fed and armed, were approaching Prague. Maximilian had promised his wife the spoils from the City. Frederick, in the meantime, still trying to organise and galvanise the army, was also bent on reassuring Elizabeth.

"I have got today two of your letters," he was writing from the army. "I entreat you not to be melancholy, and to be assured that I love you entirely. I hope God will long preserve us together, but for God's sake, take care of your health, if not out of regard for yourself, at least for the love of our dear children, and do not give way to melancholy."

He was soon urging her to leave Prague. There were rumours of possible assassination attempts, but Elizabeth adamantly refused to go. Such action would upset the Czechs and anyway she could not think of anywhere safer than Prague. Each day Frederick became more anxious about her. He wrote despairingly from the front: "I would not urge you to leave against your will. I merely give my opinion. . . . You are so bad at making up your mind."

The Imperial troops were drawing nearer. Nothing seemed to deter them: the dreadful weather, the squabbles between the two commanders, Bouquoi and Maximilian. "There are daily skirmishes," Elizabeth's loquacious new Secretary, Sir Francis Nethersole, was writing, "we can in this town hear the canon play day and night."

Bethlen Gabor was also heading for Bohemia with 10,000 men to aid Frederick.

The Queen of Bohemia reluctantly began to pack. Another winter was drawing on. If the snows came soon enough campaigning would be impossible. During the last winter the Catholics in Vienna had taunted Frederick that he would be King for only one winter— the Winter King.

Christian of Anhalt did not think the Imperial forces would attack. He had always been an optimist and this time he did have reason for hope. He knew that the enemy was a motley selection speaking a dozen different languages, difficult to organise and ridden with plague. He knew too that Bouquoi was ill.

On 8 November 1620, with the enemy encamped outside Prague, Anhalt told Frederick that there would not be a battle that day. Frederick therefore stayed inside the City, partly to see Elizabeth and partly to encourage the civilian population.

In the meantime Maximilian and Bouquoi and Tilly were debating whether or not to attack. On the whole Bouquoi thought it a bad idea, but Maximilian and Tilly instinctively felt that they should. Then a Dominican priest emerged shouting, "Fight, and ye shall prosper, in the name of the Lord of Hosts!" Maximilian had not been educated at the Catholic Ingolstadt for nothing. He immediately decided that now was the time to go into battle and he carried the army with him.

For the Bohemians the battle, fought on the White Mountain and lasting only an hour, was an ignominious defeat. Four thousand of them were killed. Many of them, practically leaderless, had retreated without putting up a fight.

Frederick had missed the decisive battle. He was on the way to rally his troops when he met Christian of Anhalt who revealed the dreadful truth. There was nothing Frederick could do but turn his horse and flee. Elizabeth was more important to him than Bohemia. Anyway Prague was practically defenceless. Everyone advised him to go. "Now I know what I am! We princes seldom hear the truth till we are taught by adversity," he said as he lifted Elizabeth into a coach. His own young life-guards saw her to the gateway of Prague and vowed that they would willingly surrender their lives on her behalf. "Never," she shouted back to them as the coach rumbled down the road, "never let our best friends have reason to curse us for the loss of their sons."

In her confusion, her efforts had been concentrated on persuading Frederick to leave as well. She had quite forgotten about her son, Rupert, and it was not until some time after the first harrowing experiences of her journey, with the gunfire sounding at the back and with the brave young men galloping at her side offering their lives in her cause, that she learnt that Baron Dhona had thrown the squalling baby into the last coach as it trundled out of the City.

Everyone forgot something. Anthalt left the state papers behind. The wagon containing Frederick's Garter insignia was waylaid by the enemy and somehow they lost the crown.

CHAPTER EIGHT

Fourteen days after leaving Prague, with the baggage being pillaged by Elizabeth's own attendants, the Cossacks fighting in the rear and the snow at last setting in, Elizabeth and Frederick reached Breslau. They had endured the first part of the gruelling and humiliating journey without complaint. When the coaches lumbered to an occasional halt Frederick could be seen wandering aimlessly in the snow pathetically wearing a bright red crumpled cloak and a jaded yellow feather in his hat. Elizabeth, who was expecting another child within a month, sat in her coach teasing her pet monkey, Jack, and joking with her attendants. Those who knew her best noticed for the first time a certain irony in some of her remarks, but she never grumbled about her circumstances or her evident physical discomfort. She did not even have a nightdress with her and, although for most of the journey she travelled in the carriage, when the road became particularly rough or the Cossacks dangerously close, she had to ride pillion with a young English volunteer, Ralph Hopton, on his horse through the snow. Her radiance, beauty and courage inspired the people who were with her and her empty title of Queen of Bohemia soon gave way to a more appropriate and permanent appellation—the Queen of Hearts.

Already Elizabeth had decided what course she would take. She was stronger and less impetuous than Céladon, as she now sometimes called Frederick after the lovesick shepherd in d'Urfée's *Astrée*. With the full force of her charm, beauty and diplomacy she hoped to regain their land and their throne.

As soon as she reached Breslau in Silesia she wrote two letters to her father: one in Frederick's name and the other in hers.

"The Baron Dhona will not fail to inform your Majesty," she wrote unwaveringly, "of the misfortune that has befallen us, and by which we have been compelled to leave Prague and come to this place, where God only knows how long we may be permitted to remain. I therefore most humbly beseech your Majesty to protect the King and myself, by sending us succour; otherwise we must be brought to utter ruin. It is from your Majesty alone next to Almighty God, that we expect assistance. I most humbly thank your Majesty for the favourable declaration you have been pleased to make respecting the preservation of the Palatinate. I eanestly entreat you to do as much for us here, and send us good aid to resist our foes; otherwise I know not what will become of us. Let me then once more implore your Majesty to have compassion on us, and not to abandon the King at the moment when he most needs assistance. As to myself, I am resolved not to leave him, and, if he must perish, why I will perish also."

Frederick felt the same about her. In fact he had worked himself into a frenzy of agitation about her forthcoming confinement. Where was she to go? He wrote rather clumsily to the Elector of Brandenburg, his brother-in-law, announcing that Elizabeth was coming to Küstrin, an old castle near Berlin. He then wrote to the Duke of Brunswick-Wolfenbüttel asking if from Küstrin Elizabeth could come on into his territory. The Elector of Brandenburg, with an eye to the Emperor, hurriedly wrote that the Castle at Küstrin was rat-infested, there was no kitchen, no furniture and it was immensely cold. In short he advised, but at the instigation of his wife did not order, her not to come. But he had reckoned without Elizabeth's stoicism and she duly installed herself in the castle to find that the Elector had only marginally exaggerated its disadvantages.

Frederick meanwhile pressed the Duke of Brunswick-Wolfenbüttel, but failed to extract a definite reply from him and Elizabeth had to resign herself to spending her fifth confinement amid the neglect and delapidation of the only refuge available.

79

"In adversity," commented Frederick sadly, "one finds few friends."

With Elizabeth comparatively safe, he had waited in Breslau in the hope of rallying some troops. Again his efforts were fruitless. The Silesians bribed him with 80,000 florins to leave their territory and Frederick declaring that "neither greed nor ambition brought us to a Bohemia", left to join Elizabeth. He told her that Ferdinand had ordered him to apologise and he had refused. His refusal might cost him the Palatinate (and protract the war), but to Frederick the whole position was still too unreal for him to be either logical or subtle. He would stand by Bohemia to the end. He had not forgotten his coronation oath.

Elizabeth gave birth to another son. "Let him be called Maurice, for he will have to be a fighter," she announced practically and diplomatically.

The Hapsburg propaganda machine was taking full advantage of Elizabeth's and Frederick's plight.

> *Ye who constantly travel over-land*, one pamphleteer asked
> *Have you not met on the highway*
> *A young man with wife and children*
> *Who was a King last winter?*
>
> *Ye Hanse Cities tell me now,*
> *Have you not arrested him?*
> *Because he owes you so much money,*
> *And does not want to pay?*

Some of them encouraged the rumour that Elizabeth had died in childbirth.

The copperplate engravings were obviously expensive and the work of experienced craftsmen. The jibes were also witty and succinct.

> *He could be made King of Lapland,*
> *There, make note, the winter is long.*

The lampoons hung on walls and fences in the most distant outposts of the Empire and beyond.

Frederick featured pathetically as "A youth fair and well-favoured excepting only a cast in one eye," who had lost his Garter insignia. Elizabeth was invariably referred to as "the Countess Palatine".

The only country which would receive Elizabeth and Frederick was Holland—or, more accurately, the United Provinces. After leaving the baby Maurice with Frederick's sister, Charlotte, who was still also housing another two young refugee Palatines and Louisa Juliana, they eventually crossed the frozen Elbe with Rupert and journeyed to Holland. They were met by the young Frederick Henry and the Dutch people, who tactfully greeted them with the same warmth which they had experienced on their wedding journey.

The United Provinces were in a state of flux. Benefiting from the truce with Spain they were amassing wealth on a vast scale from their banking operations and their commercial activities. Having wrested the lucrative Baltic trade from the Hanse towns, the Dutch sea-captains looked to wider horizons. There was money to be made in the West Indies and North America, but still more in the East. Now the Dutch were ousting the Portuguese from India, Ceylon and the islands of south-east Asia, and even pushing on to China and Japan. But Holland itself, for all its distant ventures, was the cornerstone of domesticity. It was the most advanced country in Europe and in 1620 it was entering its Golden Age. The Provinces still had the same loose organisation which had united them successfully against Spain. There was an assembly in permanent session to which they could send as many representatives as they liked, but at which each province had only one vote. To be binding on all, a decision had to be unanimous. There was also a sort of executive committee presided over by the Grand Pensionary, and then there was the Stathouder, Prince Maurice of Orange. He controlled the armed forces and by cleverly playing on the jealousies of the provinces had toppled the Grand Pensionary, Oldenbarnvelt, and installed a more pliant official in his place. He was really in control and, now that the truce had ended, was about to open a campaign aimed at conquering the Spanish Netherlands. His court untouched by elegance, betrayed no intention of rivalling those of France and England. The keynotes were simplicity, tolerance, stoicism, which were emphasised by their clean, brightly-tiled houses. Their abolition of witchhunting long before any of their European neighbours, symbolised the growing freedom of thought and scholarship. Such famous printers as the Elseviers were giving the country the reputation of being the "book-shop of Europe".

The Hague, in some ways divorced from the inland provinces, gave vent to all these characteristics. It was cosmopolitan and the numerous French and Spanish spies blended in easily with the Portuguese, English and Venetian diplomats. The larger houses were built of brick and often displayed the residents' coat of arms. Only the smallest houses in the most insignificant backstreets were thatched. The road and footpaths were scrupulously clean. Long avenues of trees, broad streets, tiny gardens and still water reflecting churches, trees or houses.

The Hague was beautiful and prosperous without being pretentious. Each street was devoted to one particular trade—Wine Harbour; Cheese Street; Glassblowers Canal—a boon to the astute Dutch housewife who, in Holland, was almost on an equal footing with her abstemious, businessminded husband. It was she who on festive occasions would ask him to dance and often it was her learning which surpassed his. Beyond the Hague stretched the cornfields, bare now that it was winter, and in the harbour were tall ships which had traversed the oceans of the world.

But the population did not always act predictably and sometimes the crowds, normally so docile behind their moss-covered walls and the well-scrubbed façades of their houses, were spurred into a mob violence which could shock Europe.

The pedestrian things of life did not appeal to Elizabeth, who thought wistfully back to one year ago. Every inch a princess, she had always enjoyed adventure and continual excitement. The atmosphere of Holland was restrained. Quieter, more impersonal, than Heidelberg, less flamboyant than Prague.

When she arrived the States installed her in a large, hastily-redecorated house on the Lange Vorhout, the Wassaenor Hof.

The exterior was a jumble of gables, dormer windows, and disproportionate roofs and chimneys. Inside there were beamed ceilings, walls hung with silk and leather, tiled floors and oak furniture. The house had been owned by the daughter of the executed Grand Pensionary Oldenbarnvelt and her exiled husband, Cornelius van der Myle. Madame van der Myle, because of her family's disgrace, was relegated to a corner of the house of which she had once been mistress.

Elizabeth, gazing out of one of the small ornate windows, hoped her stay would be short. She wanted to go to England. King James, however, already in his dotage and afraid that she might be too popular, forbade her to come. He sent £20,000 instead, for once not pausing to think that he could ill-afford it.

With Elizabeth settled, Frederick began again to think about regaining his lost territories. He was galvanised by the news which continually came to him from Bohemia. Each report was more disturbing than the last.

Among the first packages to reach Vienna from Prague had been the emotive Letter of Majesty on which the Czechs had pinned their last hopes. Ferdinand had promptly and derisively severed it with a pair of scissors and then resolved to sever by proxy the heads of the Czech leaders. Ferdinand found his inspiration in the words of the second Psalm: "Thou shalt break them with a rod of iron; thou shalt dash them in pieces like a potter's vessel." He hesitated only to acknowledge the approval of the Madonna of Loretto and then ordered the execution of the remaining leaders of the Bohemian revolt.

More bulletins arrived for Frederick and the bearers of them remained in the Hague living off their refugee King. Twenty-seven of the Czech leaders were still in Bohemia. They were rounded up, barbarously tortured and then executed in the main square of Prague. Observers reported that they displayed a courage which had been singularly lacking during the last decisive battle and their bravery and patriotism seemed potentially so infectious that the Imperial troops had had to bang drums to prevent their final words from being heard.

The next move was the expulsion of Protestant preachers and the introduction of Jesuit priests throughout the country to teach in schools and universities. The Protestant Churches were destroyed and the country ransacked. All coinage was withdrawn, reminted and returned at half its original value. Debasement of the currency, the Czechs commented wryly, was a policy begun by Frederick, whose effigy they now burnt in the streets. And still reports came of the relentless pillaging by Imperial forces and of houses and estates being confiscated. And then the refugees melted down to merely a trickle of exhausted, frightened Czechs, for behind the closed gates of Prague an orgy of sadism and brutality had made it an appropriate beginning to a war which was to be one of the most wasteful and brutal in European history.

Frederick was nauseated by what he heard. He clung to the conviction that what he had done had been right, that his motives had been pure and that he was the victim of fate. But they were tenuous convictions. The smallest word of reproof might disperse them. Reproof, that is, from those he trusted. The Catholics were very different. By now they had published the *Anhaltische Kanzlei* comprising edited extracts from the papers Anhalt had left behind in Prague. They hinted that Frederick and his adviser had intended to allow the Turks to take over Western Europe for their own ends. Although the implications were not true, they severely undermined Frederick's reputation. He reacted by publishing incriminating letters which his agents had intercepted between the Catholics. There was very little more he could do to help his cause.

King James had persuaded him to have a truce and not to act in any way without first consulting him. He had been forced to sign a humiliating document of apology to the Emperor, but hearing daily more about the destruction in Bohemia, and knowing that the Palatinate was faring little better, Frederick dreaded, and reproached himself for, each inactive day. He was almost impossible company. Continually morose, his state of mind was not helped by the bad news which was always reaching them. The Protestant Union had been disbanded; Frederick had been declared an outlaw by the Emperor; and, although half-hearted attempts were made to deter Tilly's troops, the mills of his beloved Rhineland had been taken over by the enemy and the prosperous vineyards had been ruined. . . . "They go forward," Sir Henry Wotton commented on the Spanish, "being now able to walk (while they keep a foot in the Lower Palatinate) from Milan to Dunkirk upon their own inheritances and purchases." Unleashed by Frederick's action the Spanish now had not merely secured, but reinforced a route to the Netherlands through Germany. The Thirty Years' War had inexorably begun with the two Hapsburg countries, Spain and Austria, quickly establishing their ascendancy.

Frederick could bear it no longer. He could not continue as a spectator subject to the whim of his father-in-law and a prey to terrible thoughts and forebodings. Behind King James' back he made a secret trip to Heidelberg to collect some money and valuables from his vaults. Then he set out, in April 1622, to join Mansfeld's forces in Alsace. On the way he visited incognito the court of Louis XIII and scoured Paris to buy presents which would amuse Elizabeth.

When he arrived in Alsace, a whole day was spent celebrating his arrival and the rivers became congested with boats filled with people coming to see him. Activity soon made him seem young again. He got rid of his beard and he was fired once again with youthful idealism. As usual, it was only a temporary change. Frederick, far too sensitive for the part history had had in store for him, was appalled by the behaviour of the soldiers and the terrible fate of the civilian population in the Palatinate. "Would to Heaven that there were one little corner in earth where we might dwell together in peace and contentment," he was soon writing despairingly to Elizabeth. Then Heidelberg was taken. He wrote miserably, "all sorts of atrocities have been committed there. . . . Were I to follow my own inclination I shall now become a recluse." His presence lowered the morale of the troops, who sensed his depression. Behind the beleaguered walls of Elizabeth's dower at Franckenthal an Englishman wrote: "It grieves me to behold the waste and ruin of so many towns, boroughs, and villages which were lately rich and populous, and to hear of the intolerable oppression and rapine committed upon the poor people that are left by the soldiers as well of our own army as that of the enemies. But nothing afflicts me so much as the grief wherewith the Prince [Frederick] is heavily oppressed, who suffers more than an ordinary man can undergo, for whom to trust, or whom to fly to he hardly knows."

It was to his old guardian, the Duc de Bouillon in Sedan, that he flew and there he mesmerised himself by playing tennis and swimming.

In the Hague Elizabeth tried to explain away his apparent desertion. "The prosperity the King had in the Palatinate lasted not long," she explained, "for he was constrained to leave his army (being ready to mutiny for lack of payment) and to retire to Sedan, having no help from anybody. He went thither, not without danger to his life, by the King my father's command."

Elizabeth, who had recently given birth to another child, Louisa Hollandina, had problems of her own and she was confronting them with her usual resilience. The local shop-keepers were reluctant to give her goods on credit. Her debts were continually escalating and there were many things that she still required. At least half her personal possessions, including some wedding presents, had been left behind in Prague. She hoped that they would be returned to her, but in the meantime she had to replace them and that incurred more expense.

And then of course the usual hangers-on had gathered around her: hungry and penniless representatives of the German Liberties who censoriously reproached Mansfeld for allowing his unpaid starving troops to ravish the countryside while they ate and drank all Elizabeth could secure on credit.

Moreover, the disappointed remnants of Sir Henry Vere's army were there as well, to act as a reminder of her misfortunes. "We have many volunteers here," she wrote casually to Henry's friend, Sir Thomas Roe, now Ambassador in Constantinople "so as I am never destitute of a fool to laugh at: when one goes another comes." Frequently she longed to be alone. There was hardly time to think with all the coming and going, but not everyone was unwelcome. Elizabeth's friends had also converged on the Hague. They were childhood friends from England. Lucy, daughter of the Haringtons and now Countess of Bedford and patroness of John Donne, came, and Lady Wharton as well. The English Ambassador, Sir Dudley Carleton was constantly at hand. Everyone it seemed was overflowing with loyalty and devotion, by no-one had any money. "I am ready to serve your Majesty to death, to poverty, and if you shall ever please to command, I will be converted to dust and ashes for your Majesty's sake," Sir Thomas Roe had written.

Some of the members of the Middle Temple in London kissed a sword and promised to live and die in Elizabeth's defence. And now another more daring more obsessively devoted champion had vowed to be her "knight of the lance" and to "expend all he had in the world for her". The tall thin ascetic young man, educated into the Church, wore—when he managed to get it—Elizabeth's glove in his hat and bore the name of Christian of Brunswick-Wolfenbüttel. He was the son of a great-aunt of Elizabeth's on her mother's side. Elizabeth had never met him, but that did not diminish her regard for him. She appreciated what he was doing, but such fanaticism also made her afraid for him. "It is not good in these days to be my friend," she wrote sadly, "for they ever have the worse luck." Ruthlessly and recklessly he traversed half Europe leaving in his path terrible destruction and ignoring the pleas of his more pusillanimous relations that he was fighting a useless cause. He bombarded Münster because the residents would not surrender some of Elizabeth's personal possessions which had been looted from Prague, and the money he raised from ransoms found its way back to the Palatine family in the Hague. To Elizabeth, but to few other people, he was chivalrous and honourable. Above all he was loyal. "The fault," he wrote after an important battle had been lost, "is not that of your most faithful and affectionate servant who ever loves and cherishes you."

But all this was marred by her father's attitude. However much she charmed his ambassadors and her other relations, nothing could be achieved while he refused to help. She sent him portraits of Frederick Henry and declared that she was his "obedient and loving daughter," and would always remain so. It was to no avail.

The English public were also disappointed and their feelings were expressed in a letter to King James from someone styling himself "Tom Tell-Truth".

As to the glorious Title, Defender of the Faith (which was wont to be a point of controversy between us and Rome), *the correspondent wrote*, they say flatly that your faithful subjects have more cause to question that than the Papists. . . . They that take the affairs of your children abroad most to heart, not being able to discern the compassion of your bowels, but judging things by the exterior of your actions, will hardly be persuaded that you are their father because they see the lamentable estate whereto you suffer things to run comes nearer to destruction than the nature of fatherly correction. . . . In your Majesty's own taverns for one health that is begun to yourself there are ten drunk to the Princes of foreign children.

What Elizabeth and the English public did not know was that King James had had a report compiled on the expense of sending an army to the Palatinate and had been horrified at the result. Copper ladles, shovels, sledges, kettles, ropes, master-wheelers, drummers, master-farriers, tent-keepers, a Lord Marshal and a Provost Marshal, two hundred cart-horses (which couldn't be hired but must be purchased)—it had made his head whirl. Then there were provisions, soldiers of every description to pay, powder, bullets, pieces of artillery. There was no knowing where it would end. It gave him another reason for holding back and, in James' view, a very good one. Frederick of course felt otherwise. Nothing could excuse his father-in-law's lack of support. "I shall be abandoned by everybody, and the rest of my territory given in prey to my enemies," he wrote angrily. "I cannot but be astonished to be abandoned by those who had so often promised to defend the Palatinate, without which promise, I should never have entered Bohemia. They cover all their faults by your Majesty, that you did not assist them, and they had no hopes of aid from you, perhaps for a long time. I would hope that your Majesty will show the world that you neither lack means nor good will to assist me!"

King James brushed it aside. He was tired of Frederick. His only good point was that he balanced out the Spanish marriage he still hoped to make for his son. That marriage, would in his view, resolve everything. He had become obsessed with the idea of Charles united with the sixteen-year-old sister of Philip IV of Spain. Only then, he felt, would there be hope of peace in Europe. Encouraged by the Spanish Ambassador, Gondomar—and discouraged by Parliament—James held on to the Spanish bait, little realising that secret negotiations with the Emperor Ferdinand for the hand of the Infanta were already under way. (He was also unaware that the Infanta had threatened to retire to a nunnery rather than marry a heretic.)

It was Gondomar who had persuaded James to have Sir Walter Raleigh put to death, and it was Gondomar who now convinced him that his neutrality in the war in Europe would save the Palatinate for his grandchildren. He also hinted that the Infanta would bring a dowry large enough to pay James' debts.

Although it was generally felt in England that James' money would be better spent in redeeming his mother's soul from purgatory than on treaties and negotiations with Spain, he still persisted. Moreover he forced Elizabeth to write a pleasant letter to the Infanta which enabled the Infanta, as it turned out, to snub her by failing to address her as Electress. He then sanctioned a disastrous mission to Spain headed by Endymion Porter, which was soon followed by one comprising Prince Charles and "sweet Steenie gossip", as James chose to address his favourite and his son's best friend, the Marquess of Buckingham. They travelled incognito accompanied by two friends.

It was clear that their journey was destined to be a fiasco the moment their false beards fell off as they crossed the river to Gravesend. The Infanta was angelic and pretty and Prince Charles soon imagined himself in love with her. On one occasion he, Buckingham and the bulbous Endymion Porter, resorted to climbing over a wall to catch a glimpse of her. On other occasions the Prince of Wales spent long hours in a closed coach in the street hoping to see her.

Their only achievement was in embarrassing the Spanish who, to get rid of them, proferred impossible conditions. At last, frightened for their lives and perhaps remembering Raleigh's citation of the terrible precedents when the Spaniards had used marriage as a vehicle for murder, they left bent on persuading the King to adopt an anti-Spanish policy. By the time Charles and Buckingham were wending their way back to England, it was the summer of 1623. Christian of Brunswick-Wolfenbüttel had lost an arm and duly replaced it with a silver one and Mansfeld had lost the Palatinate.

CHAPTER NINE

The atmosphere at the Palatines' Court in the Hague was more than usually depressing towards the end of 1623. King James had taken it into his head that Elizabeth had been planning to come over to England to advance her claim to the throne in case her brother was killed by the Spanish. The growing conviction in his mind that this was the truth had roused the old king to hysteria and Elizabeth and her ambassadors had had to use all their tact to calm him down. Moreover the Thirty Years' War had now blossomed into an orgy of destruction and gathering armies. What Sir Henry Wotton had described as the "fluctuation and submission" in Bohemia showed no signs of abating. In Germany the Upper Palatinate was now occupied by the Spanish, and the Lower Palatinate had been taken over by the leader of Ferdinand's army, Count Tilly. Unimpressed by a Frederick without the means to pay him, Mansfeld had for the time being gone to help the Dutch against the Spanish. The Emperor eager to place Germany under Roman Catholic hegemony had outlawed Frederick transferring his electoral dignity and lands to Maximilian of Bavaria. Almost all Protestant and even Catholic Europe disapproved of this step, but Frederick had no allies capable of opposing the Emperor and there seemed no immediate likelihood of his acquiring any.

His own initiative thwarted, Frederick had returned to the Hague. He looked so ghastly when he arrived that Elizabeth fainted at the sight of him. Bedraggled, morose, humiliated and continually complaining, he made Elizabeth bear the full brunt of his company. Nothing would absorb his attention for long. Neither the masques nor the plays which were performed in Elizabeth's court, nor the hunting trips along the Dutch coast. For hours he would sit idly and then suddenly he would throw himself into a hectic burst of inane activity. How often he repeated those words: "Now I know what I am," without for a moment comprehending his limitations and his capabilities. Pacing up and down, irascible, refusing consolation, he longed for his books, which had been removed from Heidelberg to Rome. He was irritated by the verve and continual bustle of the "largest village in Europe", which he compared unfavourably with the quiet and scholarly atmosphere of the Sedan of his childhood. His reminiscences were becoming quite tiresome. Occasionally they provoked Elizabeth into reminding him that even during their happiest days in Heidelberg he had always been discontented. No doubt, she would say sadly after hearing about his halcyon days in Sedan, he wished he had never left there. Frederick retorted that "he could have wished he had married rather a boor's daughter than the King of Great Britain's", much as he loved Elizabeth.

Not content with that, he disliked her friends. Most of them, he told her, were parasites and opportunists. Perhaps he was right. When he glanced through the letters and requests which swamped Elizabeth's writing desk, he saw evidence of continual and indiscriminate generosity.

"This letter is from Sir Oliver Cromwell, which you must answer for me, as to one that I wish very well to," she scribbled to her secretary on one acknowledgement of her kindness to the writer's children.

Even the people who saw her every day did their best to extort as many favours from her as they could. Sir Dudley Carleton had no qualms about mentioning that his wife would like her to employ her young relative, Bess, but he failed to advise her that Lady Carleton had commented that the girl was "unfashionable", "unprepossessing" and "far gone in the scurvy", which she put down to idleness. Elizabeth was evasive about this, having heard rumours about the girl, but as usual she made a point of relaying her best wishes to Lady Carleton.

Madame van der Myle, who shared the Wassaenor Hof, was the worst culprit. Elizabeth had influenced an appeal to the States to have the period of her husband's exile reduced. The result was that Cornelius van der Myle and his relatives plotted to murder the Palatines and the Stathouder. Madame van der Myle now preyed on Elizabeth's sympathy because, with the exception of her husband, who had escaped, they had paid the penalty for treason. Frederick was particularly vociferous where she was concerned, but to no avail. "I know well your custom," he accused Elizabeth bitterly, "you cannot refuse anything to anybody."

Even in her private correspondence she kept nothing from her friends. Written in her large sloping handwriting, her letters were generous in their indiscretions. The recipients did not always honour her confidences. In 1623 she was warned that she should write nothing to the Duchess of Lennox that she did not intend all the people of quality in London to know. That rumour which had so upset King James had emanated from a comment she had made in a private letter to the effect that the Spanish were hardly likely to kill her brother when she was next in line to succession. But still she continued to write, her indiscretions meandering unthinkingly over several pages. They were happy, carefree letters, seldom dwelling on her problems. "I have cause enough to be sad," she admitted to Thomas Roe," and yet I am still of my wild humour to be as merry as I can in spite of fortune."

To Frederick particularly she appeared buoyant and optimistic, but to those who understood her best her continual activity was symptomatic of deep doubt and uncertainty.

By now Frederick had submitted to what he caustically described as the "singular wisdom" of his father-in-law. He even agreed to a plan whereby Frederick Henry should marry Ferdinand's daughter, "after," as he put it in a letter to James I, "I have obtained the said full and entire restitution."

Elizabeth began to take painting lessons from the painter Honthorst and encouraged her children to do the same. A group of strolling players had just arrived in the Hague and Elizabeth often went to the Stahouder's court to watch them perform. Her father had sent her six horses to augment her stables and Elizabeth would take them out, outstripping the fastest of her companions. There were long dinner parties given by dour Dutch merchants and masques which Elizabeth sometimes found so vulgar that she felt bound to say so. With her latest child, Elizabeth's maternal instincts were, for once, aroused. "The prettiest I had," she said later. King Louis of France agreed to stand sponsor and so Elizabeth named the child after him. The other three children who were in Holland had by now moved to a house at Leyden which had been allocated to them by the Dutch States. There they were looked after by Monsieur de Plessen and his wife, who had cared for Frederick when he was a child. "Their highnesses," Sir Dudley Carleton explained in a letter, "are in part compelled to this course, by reason of the greatness of their family, which exceeds the proportion of the small house they have here." A special tutor, John Dinely, had been allocated for Prince Frederick Henry and King James had given strict instructions about how he was to be educated. "Be careful to breed him in the love of English," we wrote, "and of my people, for that must be his best living; and above all things take heed he prove not a Puritan, which is incompatible with princes, who live by order, but they by confusion."

In 1623 at the Court of Whitehall, the composer of that letter, arthritic, toothless and prematurely senile, was thinking about the future in other ways as well. History, he knew, was no longer a patchwork of unrelated events inaccurately chronicled and without form. As the seventeenth century moved forward and science evolved, precision in every field from time-keeping to reporting events became important. He minded about his place in history. His reputation with posterity mattered more to him than the views of his contemporaries, which he knew well enough. He had only to go to church to hear John Donne preaching his daughter's cause and to speak to his ambassadors to see that she had won them over too. But he wanted to be known as a peacemaker, the guardian of Europe. Only one thing mattered more than that and that was his love for his son, Charles, and his favourite, Steenie. How tiresome it was then when Prince Charles and Buckingham also continually urged him to adopt an anti-Spanish policy, to challenge that country he so feared and secretly admired, which could send her ships around the world without leaving her own waters, and whose wealth and talent were being nonchalantly frittered away with vast and useless extravaganzas. The King who had once longed for the throne of England began to dream wistfully of Spain.

Moreover the European war seemed to be advancing into another less confined stage. King James' influence was on the decline. No longer could he dither this way and that and expect all Europe to hang on his every word. Other European countries, seeing the Hapsburgs with such a strong hold in Germany, began to fear for themselves and the balance of power. The French at least diplomatically began to commit themselves on Frederick's side. Their activities in Italy succeeded in closing for the time being the passes of the Val Telline on which the Spaniards depended for moving troops from Italy to Germany.

Christian of Denmark, Elizabeth's hard-drinking, but intellectually alert, uncle, at last began to take an interest in the war. Afraid that Ferdinand's maritime policy might deprive him of the tolls paid by ships passing through the Sound, he forgot his Lutheran distaste for Calvinism and, masking his economic problems with a loathing for Roman Catholicism, he joined the fray. Events proved that he had fatally misjudged the enemy.

Gustavus Adolphus of Sweden was also taking a keen interest. But he wanted cash in advance for his help and King James, with his perpetual financial difficulties, was in no position to meet him. So Gustavus went off to fight the Poles. On the other hand, Bethlen Gabor, who had never been in the right place at the vital moment, was negotiating with the Emperor and this despite all Sir Thomas Roe's efforts from Constantinople to bring him in on the Protestant side. The Spanish had already attempted to invade the United Provinces and only the weather and lack of supplies had stopped them succeeding.

Tired, old and doting, James was being bullied by his heir and his favourite to protect his children's honour and regain the Palatinate.

And so for Elizabeth and Frederick, the war was nothing if not unpredictable, and with the spring of 1624 came new hope. News came from England that Prince Charles was planning to marry Henrietta Maria, sister of the French King in order to secure an Anglo-French alliance against the Hapsburgs. As a gesture of goodwill Elizabeth sent her mother, Marie de Medicis, two small dogs. Mansfeld as a Protestant was being welcomed by the people of London like a hero in the old style and Parliament reflected the feelings of the British people by voting money for the restoration of the Palatinate. Elizabeth now indulged herself in the hope that they would soon be returning to Heidelberg. She imagined one swift campaign expelling the Spanish from the Palatinate and banishing the Emperor's men from Bohemia. Her confidence was infectious and for a time even Frederick shared it.

By June France and the United Provinces had signed a treaty of friendship, which England soon joined. This was something Elizabeth had been working towards for some time. Sweden and Denmark agreed to sink their differences in a common aim, and the Elector of Brandenburg ceased his neutrality and joined the United Provinces.

But King James' preparations for war against Spain were, as Elizabeth put it in August, moving "but slowly forward". The press gangs set about their job in the backstreets of London and collected nearly 12,000 unwilling "volunteers". They set off to Holland, but were not allowed to land. The plague resulting from cramped quarters, rotten food and foul water on shipboard, killed nearly half of them. Eventually, when the survivors staggered ashore and marched off to relieve Breda, they were too late: the town had fallen to the Spanish.

As usual as winter approached Elizabeth provided an addition to her family. Edward, as he was called, was a new candidate for the nursery at Leyden. Elizabeth dispatched him to the care of Frederick's old governess, Madame de Plessen, as soon as possible.

Four deaths quickly following each other, marred the winter and the spring. The Duc de Bouillon; Louis, the child Elizabeth had borne the year before, and Maurice the Stathouder, all died. More significantly, on 27 March 1625, the son of Mary Queen of Scots breathed his last. He had always been ailing, but he had survived for so long against all the odds that no-one had really expected him to die now. Perhaps he would not have done so had he not insisted on drinking enormous quantities of beer in the mistaken belief that that would effect a cure, and then ordering a special brew from Buckingham's mother which finally put an end to his sufferings.

His body lay in state appropriately surrounded by Spanish candlesticks. The hearse that carried him through London had been designed by Inigo Jones. It was the end of an era.

The accession of "baby Charles" to the English throne raised Elizabeth's hopes. Frederick's secretary, Rusdorf, had suggested that she should go to England at once to rally support, but Elizabeth would not comply. Such a gesture, she argued, might indicate distrust and there was nothing to justify that. Was not Charles the brother who had thrown himself at his father's feet pleading with him to help her? When James had refused, had he not retired to his room for two days weeping? He had sent her all the money he possessed. She visualised the sweet, adoring brother of twelve years ago. Not for a moment did she guess at the obstinacy which had resulted from his lonely sickly childhood or, that behind his delicate features was a corresponding feminity, a belief in intuition and an impetuousity which could be ruled by nothing, except sometimes the whim of Buckingham. They were weak foundations on which to build any hopes, but at first Charles did try to be worthy of his sister's trust.

Instilled with a feeling of romance and spurred on by an idealised view of Elizabeth, he promised to send armies to recover the Palatinate and Bohemia. When the Spanish questioned him about his warlike activities, he meaningfully reminded them that the Queen of Bohemia now had a King for a brother.

Elizabeth wrote delightedly to Sir Thomas Roe: "My brother doth shew so much love to me in all things as I cannot tell you how much I am glad of it." She felt that the cynics had been proved wrong. Charles had not failed her. By now Sir Henry Vane, "Vanity" as Elizabeth called him, had arrived at the Hague. He assured Elizabeth again of Charles' love and devotion for her and spoke to her of an English subsidy of £20,000 a month on top of the £46,000 her brother had already sent.

Having dealt with Elizabeth, Sir Henry then began to look at the Court of the Hague. It was certainly a happier place than the Court at Whitehall where the feeling of indolence, decadence and seediness instilled into it by James I still pervaded. The Court at the Hague was becoming more frivolous and less like an army quartering station than it had been when he had last been there. The cause of this transformation was quite obvious. Frederick Henry, the new Stathouder, had married Amalia de Solms. "She is handsome and good," Elizabeth had said. She was also beautiful and lively. The Court at the Binnenhof now revolved around her.

Holland was approaching her Golden Age and for once history had been kind to her. William the Silent, the visionary hero; Maurice the soldier, and now Frederick Henry, dynastically more ambitious and artistic, had come in the right order. Already Maurice was nearly forgotten, but Elizabeth in the Wassaenor Hof was deeply disturbed by his death. "A friend," she wrote of him, "whom I loved as a father." Little did she know that his death was to be the cause as well as the forerunner to even profounder griefs. But four difficult years would pass before those tragedies began to unfold. In the meantime Elizabeth was grateful to Maurice for bequeathing her shares in a Dutch shipping company and the younger children at Leyden, prancing like unschooled colts, despite their rigorous training, would play a game called "What Shall We Do When the Ships Come In?" Watching them would be their gentler, less tempestuous older brother, Frederick Henry. One stormy afternoon he had cut with a diamond the words *Mediis tranquillus in Undis* on the crystal ship Prince Maurice had given him as a christening present. He was growing up. Elizabeth often commented on his resemblance to the long-dead Henry. By the time he was eight he could speak French, English, Italian, German and Czech fluently and was persisting with his Latin. He was a prodigy, just as Henry had been. "I shall marry my mother," he had announced flatteringly one day as he watched Elizabeth lead the hunt in a brightly coloured hat. But the Duke of Buckingham had quite different ideas, which had been fostered by his enemies. He wanted Frederick Henry to marry his daughter, Lady Mary Villiers. He believed it would be another step in his quick ascent to power. He wrote to Elizabeth about it nonchalantly enough not to rewrite a page when he had scored out and corrected whole sentences and carelessly splodged the paper with ink.

In the spring he came to the Hague. His hair immaculately cut and curled, charming and elegant. He impressed the Dutch people as much as he secretly impressed Elizabeth and more blatantly her children. It was nice to see grandeur again. His clothes and possession showed an almost refreshing disregard for cost. His visit to Holland, however, had other motives apart from those of diplomacy and one day, without anyone knowing, he slipped away to Amsterdam with the English crown jewels and pawned them on Charles's behalf.

When he came back, he spoke to Elizabeth of the wealth of England and about the things which would be done to restore her to her rightful position. He lavished presents on her and her family and spoke of armies and sometimes, in charmingly unguarded moments, of the Court of France, which he so much admired. Elizabeth was uncertain of him. She was, however, delightful to him. She had never tried harder. He was after all, as she disparagingly commented one day "more important than Charles it seems". Buckingham in return gave more and more promises. And so as the spring of 1625 merged into summer, Elizabeth and Frederick could go on a happy trip around the Dutch countryside, full of optimism.

But already astute observers in England were remarking that the promises Buckingham had given to his King's sister could never be fulfilled. Besides anything else, the omens, always so accurate where the Stuarts were concerned, were against them now. In England in 1625, 35,428 people died of the plague. It was the worst epidemic anyone could recall—three times as bad as the last major outbreak in 1603, the year King James had come to the throne. In August Charles stopped Parliament expressing its dislike of

Buckingham by dissolving it and it was clear that, like all the Stuarts, he had already overestimated his own influence. Neither he nor Buckingham had the power to pursue the foreign policy geared to Elizabeth's welfare. That power was vested in Parliament, not in the Crown. He must first negotiate with Parliament, for it was they who held the purse-strings.

More ominously for Elizabeth, it was soon to be Charles' French Catholic wife who held his heart. She was nowhere near doing so yet, it was true. Charles and Henrietta Maria were scarcely on speaking terms. Lonely, bigoted, almost ugly, the child of Henry of Navarre and Marie de Medici could not compete with the mellifluous urbanity of Buckingham.

By the end of the year very little had been achieved for the Protestant cause, either in England or on the continent. Surely, thought Elizabeth in the Hague, as she read the reports of failed campaigns and incalculable human misery, it could not get any worse. But she was not sure.

"Our cousin the young Duke of Brunswick," began the postscript to a letter she had just dispatched to her brother, "hath been very sick but he is upon recovery." It was on him that Elizabeth pinned her hopes. There was a letter from Prince Christian's brother on her desk. Slowly she scanned it. It informed her that "after the suffrance of a cruel fever lasting some fourteen or more days", Christian had died. The shock robbed Elizabeth of her "wild humour". It was the last thing she had expected. It had chiefly been Christian's optimism which had instilled into her that unnatural state of hope. Recently she had come to rely on it more and more. Nothing now was left but a brooch he had bequeathed to her and which she had converted to a bracelet and was to wear for the rest of her life. Her glove, in which he had vowed to bring back the Palatinate, lay abandoned in Rhineland mud. The Catholics circulated a rumour that, like Herod, Christian's entrails had been devoured by an enormous worm. And so the most fanatical champion of the Protestant cause, the twenty-seven-year-old Christian of Brunswick-Wolfenbüttel, was laid to rest.

With a feeling of acute despair, Elizabeth turned to Frederick. No-one else was left, she felt, to pursue their cause. Charles had achieved nothing. A meeting between Frederick's representatives and the Emperor's, arranged by the English King, proved a fiasco and left an aggrieved Frederick, "saddened almost to death". It would have been better to have done nothing at all.

Christian of Denmark must have been feeling the same way, too. Danish intervention had proved a disaster. In the end it had given Ferdinand a new ally and with him a new reason to hope.

He was Albert von Wallenstein, a brilliant opportunist soldier of fortune. He was also a Catholic convert and as unscrupulous as he was dependent on astrology. Through the vehicle of a judicious marriage and the exploitation of Ferdinand's policy of selling the confiscated land in Bohemia, he now owned half of the Czech lands. Acquisitive for power, he had decided to make himself useful to Ferdinand. And so he offered the Emperor 50,000 troops. Ferdinand, wary of private armies and distrustful of Wallenstein, opted for 20,000.

This army had come marching out of Bohemia and when Mansfeld had advanced to deal with this new threat, he had been repulsed and forced to retreat eastwards. This had given the Imperialists their chance and Tilly had crushed the Danes at Lütter.

Mansfeld meanwhile had sought the aid of Bethlen Gabor, with Wallenstein hot on his heels. Gabor had always been a lukewarm supporter of the Protestant cause, and he was taking no risks this time. Mansfeld got no help from him. With a handful of men he set off again, probably hoping to take service with Venice, a resolute opponent of the Hapsburgs in Italy. He never got there, and died that bitter November on a hillside above Sarajevo. With all the faults of a mercenary captain, he had still served the Protestant cause, and many thought his death a grievous loss.

Elizabeth thought so too. The fluctuations of her hopes had served no useful purpose for her and were beginning to tell on her health. The child she bore that year was weak and sickly. She tactfully and quickly, because of the child's weakness, had her christened Henrietta Maria. Then Elizabeth retired to the precincts of the Wassaenor Hof pleading the birth as an excuse for not going out. The real reason was that, for once, she couldn't face the world. With her mounting debts (she owed, for instance, £554 to the chandler, £478 to the baker and large amounts to nearly every other form of tradesman) and Charles's marriage with the probability eventually of direct heirs, Elizabeth's prestige in the Hague was diminishing. Now that Sir Dudley Carleton had gone to London, as it turned out only temporarily, to be Vice-Chamberlain to King Charles, she tended to be left out of negotiations and discussions. For Elizabeth the snubs were all the more difficult to bear because it was her lady-in-waiting who was now in the ascendant. Amalia now had a son and the Orange family's standing was higher than ever. Elizabeth bore her no real grudge. It was simply that she regarded her as a parvenu. Despite her apparently liberal education, Elizabeth was a child of Tudor England. She did not like or tolerate the new aristocracy which was dependent more on wealth and trade than on royal patronage. In an age which was questioning fundamental precepts, when premises as firmly rooted as the world being the centre of the universe was being challenged, Elizabeth and Frederick believed absolutely in the Divine Right of Kings—but only kings with a long lineage of rulers behind them. That "one of my women" should parade as something verging on a princess was repugnant to her. Amalia, it was true, treated Elizabeth with the same deference that she always had done. She respected the old order too. But there was no hiding the truth; no denying that when, for instance, the artist Rubens came to the Hague to try and secure peace between England and Spain as an ambassador for the Archduchess Isabella it was to the Stathouder's Court at the Binnenhof that he went. The Wassaenor Hof, with its faded hangings, was out of fashion. Elizabeth too was not feeling her best. She summoned a doctor and asked him to prescribe some treatment which would cure her. She would, she told him, agree to be bled if necessary, but under no circumstances would she take any medicine—something she had always disapproved of and done very well without.

The feeling of gloom from the Wassaenor Hof permeated even the nursery at Leyden. "I trust you omit not to pray diligently," wrote the brilliant and angelic Frederick Henry to his brother Charles Louis in Brandenburg, "as I do both day and night, that it may please God to restore us to happiness and to each other. I have a bow and arrow with a beautiful quiver, tipt with silver, which I would fain send you, but I fear it may fall into the enemy's hands."

Soon after he received that letter, Charles Louis was preparing to go to Holland. He was a small swarthy boy, diffident, but determined. The years away from his parents had hurt him deeply and he defied this by appearing insensitive and intractable. His sister, Elizabeth, with her statuesque appearance and great learning, was also reserved. She did not want to leave her grandmother, to whom she was devoted. Maurice, who was only seven, thought of nothing but the excitement of the journey. Wallenstein's troops were stationed in Brandenburg and the country the children were to traverse was plague-ridden. Moreover they would be useful to the enemy as hostages. Bringing Frederick's children across Germany would be hazardous.

In the event nothing untoward happened and the children arrived at the Hague safely. It was with some trepidation that they prepared to meet their parents. They must be careful, they were warned, not to upset the King and Queen. Elizabeth and Maurice were too careful. Their mother greeted them warmly, but when they were out of the room she remarked cuttingly that here in the young Elizabeth was another Louisa Juliana and in Maurice a shadow for Rupert. About Charles Louis she said nothing. His dark wilfulness disconcerted and yet fascinated her. Day after day there were verbal conflicts, but she could never be quite sure of their outcome. Charles Louis was not afraid of her as her other children were and it was reluctantly that she sent him with his brother and sister to Leyden. There was no alternative. Yet another pregnancy was drawing to a close. Confined to the house, she amused herself by poring over the catalogue of the books at the Frankfurt Fair that year and playing with her dogs and monkeys. "When your gentleman with the moustachios comes," she wrote to Thomas Roe, anticipating Turkish addition to her menagerie, "he shall be very welcome and shall inherit old Jack's place." There were other domestic details to preoccupy her as well. "I pray send me," she continued in the same letter, "as soon as you can some store of the musk melon seed that grew at Constantinople. The old Count of Tour brought some hither that grows very well and it is a fruit that I love exceedingly."

The child that year was called Philip. Like Charles Louis, he was dark and strong. No sooner had he joined the other children and Elizabeth had recovered from a bout of measles than Frederick was suffering from another serious bout of melancholia. The refugees from Bohemia were still converging on the Hague. They spoke of barbarity, torture and exile. Ferdinand had made his son the hereditary King of Bohemia; had suppressed Protestantism completely and was now destroying the Czech culture. Sixty thousand books had been burnt. The German language was being introduced. All these facts, Frederick masochistically gleaned from the Czechs who thronged the Hague. The ones who had seen him in Prague hardly recognised him. Frederick at thirty was a broken old man. No-one but Elizabeth took him seriously any more. Even his children were more in awe of their mother than of their father. That they loved him more was quite a different matter and a fact that Frederick never noticed. It did not cross his mind. Totally humiliated, consistently undervalued, it amazed him that Elizabeth still loved him. That she continued to try and rouse him, also surprised him. But she did, feigning optimism at every reversal. When Buckingham was assassinated in 1628 she diplomatically expressed regret and then confided to Frederick that she now hoped her brother would really devote himself to their cause without being impeded by Buckingham. In fact Buckingham had, for his own selfish reasons, supported her cause and his death would not in any way assist the Palatines.

Frederick tried to respond to Elizabeth's efforts, but there was seldom any good news these days. When it did come, he was momentarily confident that their luck was turning. The ship the children had talked about for so long, had come in. A Spanish galleon with plate worth £870,000 on board, had been captured by the company Elizabeth had shares in. One eighth of the booty was due to her. They began to talk of honouring their debts. The ship was anchored in the Zuyder Zee. Frederick resolved to go and collect Elizabeth's share at once and Frederick Henry, who was having a military education in the Hague, begged to be allowed to go as well.

Looking happier than he had for months, Frederick set off on the journey. Father and son travelled by packet-boat. They made their claim and then began the return journey. The river was over-crowded with boats full of drunken Dutchmen, who were visiting the treasure. It was a cold misty night and, as they were passing Harlem Meer, a cargo vessel rammed their packet-boat.

The packet-boat began to sink. In the turmoil the passengers fought one another trying to get out. The skipper, more sober than the rest, swam to the retreating cargo-boat shouting that the King of Bohemia must be saved. Frederick was dazed and bruised. Somehow he had become separated from his son and was hardly aware as he moved over to the other ship that he was no longer with him. Only as the boat drew away did he see Frederick Henry climb up to the mast and hear him shout, "Father! Save me, father!" Frantically Frederick tried to dive into the water, but he was forcibly restrained. The boat retreated into the damp fog. Later that night he returned to the place where they had left the boat, but he achieved nothing. In the morning Frederick Henry's corpse was found, frozen to the mast.

CHAPTER TEN

Night after night, tossing and turning in his bed, unable to sleep, those words "Father! Save me, father," haunted Frederick. He would feel again the cold mist on his face, hear the panic-stricken voices in the darkness and then those words would cut a stillness across the confusion. They never left him. Slowly, remorselessly they were to drive him to his grave.

Even in breaking the news to Elizabeth he had failed. She had been nursing her three-week-old daughter, Charlotte. Frederick had not dared to break the news to her himself. Instead he had asked her friend, Lord Carlisle, to tell her. The shock, her servants reported, nearly killed her.

A melancholy stillness fell over the house. Despite the proceeds of the Spanish galleon, the Palatines could not raise enough money to pay for Frederick Henry's funeral. Dressed in mourning paid for by their uncle, Rupert, Maurice and the young Elizabeth, watched over the embalmed body of their brother and ensured that the flowers which surrounded him were fresh and the candles renewed. Elizabeth in another room sifted through the interminable letters of condolence. There was certainly no shortage of sympathy.

"Everyone hath his appointed time to live," quoted Daniel Souterius in his book dedicated to Elizabeth on the death of her son.

> *Here lies perhaps a Prince; yet who can tell?* Sir Thomas Roe wrote,
> *So like he was an angel . . .*
> *Now he is not; we wonder what he was,*
> *Rich as a diamond yet as frail as glass.*

Had he known of the crystal ship, Frederick Henry's prize possession, which as it turned out, had been so ominous, Sir Thomas might have avoided that analogy. However, Elizabeth read it, no doubt reminding herself that the room in the Wassaenor Hof where Frederick Henry was lying was not really good enough. She had never been sentimental about the trappings of death. She found effigies such as the one on William the Silent's tomb of his loyal spaniel more irritating than moving. King Charles wanted his nephew to be buried at Delft with the Princes of Orange. Elizabeth, however, argued that, if her son were buried there it would involve an expensive funeral procession. That she could not afford. It would be much better for him to be interred in the Cloister Church in the Hague and even that was only made financially feasible by King Charles pawning his personal jewels to raise the money. At last Frederick Henry's body was moved across the road to the Cloister Church. There each chime of the bells would serve to remind his family of their loss, and particularly to Frederick. He was too distracted to give the funeral arrangements much attention. "It is," he explained to his brother-in-law, "a grief that no pen can express." But his face expressed his feelings well enough. He never smiled. Continually forlorn, holding himself completely responsible, Elizabeth had to rouse herself in order to comfort him.

As soon as they could they left the Hague for Rhenen. There Frederick was supervising the building of a palace. "A neat palace or country house," John Evelyn was to record in his diary a decade later, "built after the Italian manner as I remember." Frederick now dreamt of leading a bucolic existence with his wife and family. All the money he could raise was spent on this idyllic project. Elizabeth sold some of her menagerie; Sir Francis Nethersole sold some of the plate which had been a present to him from the French King and still the Italian Palazzo in the green fields overlooking the Rhine was not able to have the benefit of first-rate building materials. Moreover, when the foundations had already been built and the walls were creeping higher and higher under Frederick's instructions, news came that the Palatines' pensions were in jeopardy. Charles in England had abandoned Parliament, thus unwittingly tightening the purse-strings.

The full implications were not apparent to Elizabeth. Sir Thomas Roe, returning to England overland from his embassy in Constantinople, had called at Rhenen to see her. Of course she had discussed all this with him, telling him how she was busily contriving to have Frederick Henry's pension of £2,000 a year transferred to Charles Louis and Rupert. Frederick was more aware of the problems as he fumbled through bills for servants' liveries, for portraits and for food. Soon he was announcing dramatically that he would have to send Elizabeth to England to throw herself at the mercy of her brother because he, her husband, "was not able to put bread into her mouth."

As time went by Frederick began to suffer not only from melancholy, but also from bouts of hysteria. There was an excuse, however, and one which was being whispered in every court in Europe. From the Hofburg in Vienna, to the Doge's Palace in Venice, the news was spreading that Frederick V of the Palatinate was dying. In his slow Scots accent King Charles of England ordered his ambassadors to urge his brother-in-law to pull himself together and look after his health, if only for the sake of his family. Elizabeth in her hurried handwriting tried to dispel the rumours. They simply were not true, she declared. "The King," she affirmed, "here hath been evil first of a sore throat and since of a weakness which took away his stomach, but after that an imposture or two broke out upon his body. He is well again and I hope will be abroad at Easter." But the rumours still persisted, even when Frederick did join the Prince of Orange's army against the Spanish shortly after Easter. The recklessness with which he often expressed himself in words was now transferred to the battlefield. "I have seen His Majesty," Thomas Roe was soon writing to Elizabeth, "without sense of an enemy, look upon them and I beseech you to prevent that he look not too much. . . . Madam, I cannot say enough of him; he is a most brave, sad, just and obliging prince."

"Brave, sad, just" perhaps, but Sir Thomas soon discovered that Frederick was not "obliging". He might salute King Charles' wisdom, and goodness and declare that he entirely depended on those qualities in his brother-in-law. Nevertheless he was so querulous that Sir Thomas soon felt unable to confront him and he asked Elizabeth to act as an intermediary between him (as the King of England's servant) and her husband.

In fact Frederick at the front was proving as troublesome as Frederick at home. Time and again Elizabeth found herself soothing her brother's ambassadors, who considered they had been affronted by Frederick and each day, hearing reports of Frederick's foolhardiness on the battlefields, she became more concerned about his personal safety. It was with an added sense of relief that she learnt that the campaign in the Netherlands was a success and Frederick was coming home. He arrived in time for them both to witness the departure of the besieged Spanish garrison from Bois-le-Duc. Sitting in a tent they watched the half-starving men, women, children, monks and nuns, limping, weeping, dressed in rags, defiling out of the town. The victims were suffering from the usual diseases concomitant with a besieged town and Elizabeth managed to contract a severe fever. After a short visit to the Hague she went to Rhenen "to air" herself, as she put it. There, surrounded by seemingly inanimate streams and grazing cattle, the two convalescents—one whose health would weather almost any storm and the other masking as best he could a dry consumptive cough— read in peace the deciphered reports of events in Germany. They had heard from Sir Thomas Roe, who had spent some of the summer with them, that the devastation and agony continued in the Palatinate. "I hear nothing but lamentations," he had reported, "nor see variety but of dead bodies."

Now, when the Protestant cause seemed at its lowest ebb, Ferdinand was induced, perhaps by the machinations of the French, to give his fanaticism full rein. Wallenstein had completed the defeat of the Danes. He dominated North Germany and had pushed his conquests to the Baltic. His one failure had been against the Hanse port of Stralsund, and this was ominous for the future, for a Swedish force had raised the siege.

Nevertheless Ferdinand felt strong enough to show his hand and issue an Edict of Restitution. All property which had been secularised since 1552 was to revert to the Catholic Church. This was a flagrant contravention of the aims of the Treaty of Augsburg. The territorial rights of the Princes of Northern Germany were threatened. The Emperor had gone too far. Up until that time the German Princes had sought to remain neutral. Now there was nothing more for them to do but fight it out. They could not do that alone. In fact they hardly had enough energy to choose a leader. However, they did have enough energy to meet at Regensburg in open revolt against the Edict and in protest against the way in which Wallenstein's power and possessions seemed constantly to be on the increase.

Ferdinand in a way shared their suspicions and agreed to dismiss Wallenstein. He also had to accept for the time being their revolt over the Edict. He had other matters on his mind.

Now that the Huguenot revolt had been suppressed and La Rochelle had fallen, France was free to continue her feud with the Hapsburgs, and this she did by supporting a French claimant to the Duchy of Mantua. Ferdinand, therefore, took his eye off Germany and transferred Imperial troops to Italy at a time when both were needed in the north. For Richelieu, in a devious move, patched up Sweden's quarrel with Poland, leaving the former free to come to the aid of the Protestant Princes. And so from across the Baltic Sea came another Scandinavian, more brilliant, more belligerent, and perhaps more self-seeking than the Danish King. The Thirty Years' War moved into another phase.

Gustavus Adolphus was the most exceptional man of his age. Ever since he could remember he had listened in on meetings with Government officials and foreign ambassadors. At six he had gone on a military campaign with his father. At seventeen he had come to the Swedish throne, on which his dynasty, the House of Vasa, had sat insecurely since 1523. He was an avowed Lutheran. He was a linguist. He loved art, and was an accomplished lutenist. His charm and good looks were proverbial. His myopia, which was to prove fatal in the end, gave him a scholarly expression. He was ambitious, easily provoked, but kind when he wanted to be. He was courageous as well, thinking nothing of riding into battle without armour. Above all he was a natural leader of men and that, with his genius for fighting and for understanding every facet of war from strategy to medical care, accounted for the history of military successes in wars against Denmark, Russia and Poland that lay behind him.

The Protestants in Germany now looked to Sweden with a mixture of distrust and hope. They joked among each other about Laplanders and Finns who did not see light in winter or darkness in summer. Secretly they were afraid of such unusual phenomena, but they were comforted by the fact that, if the Swedes were coming, they were on the Protestant side. Frederick, who was related to Gustavus through his sister's marriage saw a glimmer of hope in the future. Louisa Juliana had already welcomed the Swedish King in Berlin.

Only Charles in England seemed to take no notice. He was pressing for peace with Spain. Sir Henry Vane assured Elizabeth that the peace would not be concluded "without our full restitution", and Charles wrote ambiguously of "those physics which men call benigna medicamenta; which if they do no good, shall do no hurt." Nevertheless, as the negotiations proceeded, it became increasingly clear to the diplomats of Europe that the Palatines' cause was hardly an issue at all. King Charles, his hair already showing traces of grey, his expression more aloof and solemn, saw little resemblance in the painting Honthorst had done of Elizabeth being received by Diana and Apollo to the girl who had cried at the thought of leaving her family and going to Germany. As he looked at the picture there was an unpleasant suspicion that even that had not been paid for. "The grey mare," as he had once rudely referred to her, had been replaced, in that corner of his heart reserved for women, by his wife.

Nevertheless he could not shake her off just like that. She was too popular in England for one thing and for another she was his only sister and he was conscious of family obligations.

Besides Charles had a long-standing dislike of Spain and could still, perhaps, be dissuaded from coming to terms. In his Court now was the painter Rubens. The Spaniards knew how susceptible the young King was to art. They remembered how impressed he had been with the Spanish collections when he had made his ridiculous visit to Spain. And so Rubens brought a painting with him. It was called "Allegory on the Blessings of Peace." It contrasted the advantages of peace with the devastations of war. It was a beautiful picture, and as such much more persuasive than the skilfully worded letters which came so frequently from his "only dear sister" in the Hague. Elizabeth promptly despatched Rupert and Maurice to Whitehall hoping they would somehow redress the balance.

"I hear the treaty with Spain goeth on," Elizabeth was writing in March to the Earl of Carlisle, "you know my mind, that I am still incredulous that they will do anything, except it be upon dishonourable conditions."

She was right and when the news did come of the terms of the peace that was being made with Spain, Elizabeth was prepared for it. "Thou ugly filthy Camel's face," she taunted Carlisle, who had had a part in the negotiations: ". . . I confess I am not much rejoiced at it, yet I am so confident of my dear brother's love, and the promise he hath made me, not to forsake our cause, that it troubles me the less. I must desire your sweet face to continue your help to us, in this business which concerns me so near; and, in spite of you, I am ever constantly, Your most affectionate friend, Elizabeth."

Frederick, who had long given up all pretence of good humour, burst into tears in the presence of Henry Vane and had to be forcibly restrained from attacking the fat ambassador, who relayed an unfavourable report of the meeting to his monarch in England. This provoked Charles into telling Elizabeth some home-truths. "And first give me leave to tell you," he began, "that it is impossible in this unfortunate business of yours either to give or take a Counsel, in itself, absolutely good; And whosoever makes you believe otherwise, deceives you."

It had taken King Charles ten years to appreciate the facts. Now he had relinquished idealism for what he might have regarded as realism and what Frederick no doubt regarded as downright treachery. By now Frederick had been forced to resign his claims in the Palatinate in favour of Charles Louis. In exchange for this compromise the imperial ban had been revoked and Frederick was granted an income from some of the Palatine territories. As usual he had been desperate for money. Very little of the pensions and allowances which came from England for Elizabeth and Frederick ever reached them. More often than not they were intercepted by unscrupulous creditors and, as their standing in England and Holland declined, it was becoming progressively more difficult for them to do anything about it. Their hopes for the future had been diminished by the birth of a direct heir to the throne of England. In 1629 Henrietta Maria had borne a child which had only survived two hours. In King Charles' words, he had chosen to save the mould rather than the cast. Now Frederick was being asked to be god-father to another son, Charles. "The son of our love", as Charles I later referred to him, was, in the words of his mother, "so ugly that I am almost ashamed to own him". "The nurses told me," reported the Venetian Ambassador enthusiastically, "that after his birth he had never clenched his fists, but had always kept his hands open. From this they augur that he will be a prince of great liberality."

Bonfires were lit in the streets, cannons were fired and the planet Venus shone that morning with unusual radiance. The Palatines loyally celebrated and letters were dispatched from Elizabeth and Charles Louis.

The birth in England caused considerably more of a stir even in the Hague than the birth of another daughter to Elizabeth in October. She was called Sophia after her great-grandmother on her mother's maternal side. She was the Palatines' twelfth child and Henrietta Maria would bear eight children. Nevertheless one day she would be heir to the throne of England and it would be her child, George I, who would sit on the English throne. But that would be after Amalia de Solms' grandchild, William of Orange, had vacated it and Sophia's child would bring to the throne of England, which he had reached through such a circuitous course, none of the charm of his grandmother (or his mother), or indeed of the squalling infant who now lay in the arms of Henrietta Maria in

St James's Palace. "Being the twelfth child of the King my father," wrote Sophia years later, "and of the Queen my mother, I can well believe that my birth caused them but little satisfaction, except a feeling of relief at my vacating the place I had until then occupied." She was quickly moved to the strictly regulated court at Leyden, while her family went into mourning for her sister, Charlotte.

Had Elizabeth known that Amalia de Solms' grandchild would be King of England before hers, she would hardly have been pleased. Snubs and affronts were becoming the norm for her and Frederick now. Far from the problems of etiquette being resolved, they had become increasingly more complicated. So much time was spent in maintaining their position as a king and queen and in anticipating every slight and avoiding it. When César de Vendôme, the bastard son of Henri IV of France, was passing through the Hague en route to see Gustavus Adolphus, he could not pay the Palatines an official visit since France had not recognised Frederick as King of Bohemia. Instead he tried to visit them unofficially at ten o'clock in the morning, when, as it turned out, they were both still in bed. When Frederick heard about it he announced that he would only accept an official visit and Elizabeth wrote diplomatically to Vendôme saying that she and Frederick were just setting off for Rhenen and could not see him.

The new French Ambassador was less indulgent than Vendôme. Indeed de Hauterive was so hostile towards Elizabeth and Frederick that ultimately his government felt obliged to recall him. In Vienna it was reported that English diplomats were making similarly disparaging remarks which went unchecked by their mentors in Whitehall. The general antagonism was emphasised when the Duchess of La Tremouille, Frederick's aunt, arrived for Prince Charles's christening and was no longer treated as a princess of the blood as she had been in the past. In true Palatine fashion, she angrily left London on the same day as the christening.

Each day the position got worse. Elizabeth and Frederick were insulted by shopkeepers and in the streets lampoons were distributed about their straitened circumstances. Even in Church they were mocked at. One Sunday the preacher accused them of "revelling" at a masque which had taken place on a national day of mourning. Frederick rose from his pew and harangued the preacher for various misdemeanours he was said to have committed. The congregation objected to this and Frederick was forced to sit down while the preacher unctuously resumed his sermon.

Such snubs were demoralising for Elizabeth and, as she grew older, the humdrum commercialism of the Hague began to take its toll, not only on her figure but also on her resilience. Consequently, subconsciously, she came to rely more on Frederick to flatter and reassure her. Each time he went away she longed more eagerly for his return. Her ladies-in-waiting began to dread the days when no post could be expected. On those days Elizabeth would invariably seem distracted and depressed. She never doubted of course that Frederick would return, nor did she ever allow herself to give up hope that their cause would reach a successful conclusion.

Their mutual hopes were now with Gustavus Adolphus. Elizabeth wrote to her brother urging him to support the genius from Sweden. She protested, and almost threatened, that if Gustavus Adolphus should fail them then "we shall never have anything, but live to be a burden to you, and a grief and affliction to ourselves and posterity."

But he did not look like failing. The Imperialists' reaction to Gustavus's entry into the war had been to sack Magdeburg with such slaughter and brutality that it drove the wavering Protestant princes into the Swedish camp. Gustavus had then soundly thrashed the Catholic armies at Breitenfeld and, leaving his Saxon allies to take care of Bohemia, had marched across Germany to the Rhine.

Frederick was naturally more eager to help. He wrote encouragingly to Gustavus Adolphus offering himself as a volunteer. The Swedish King, anxious to avoid the stigma of a foreign invader who had come merely to expand territorially, asked Frederick to join his forces. Frederick only waited for the birth of his thirteenth child before setting off. The child was born on 2 January 1632. He had wanted to christen him Frederick Henry, but Elizabeth insisted that he should be called Gustavus after the Palatinate's new hero. Someone commented that the Winter Queen had started on her second dozen, but, in fact, Elizabeth, generous as always, was merely rounding off a baker's dozen.

It was on 16 January 1632 that Frederick, accompanied by a young Englishman, Lord Craven, left the Hague for the front. Full of hope, he told Elizabeth that he would soon be sending for her to join him in Heidelberg. "The setting sun rises again" was the motto Elizabeth selected for the latest medallion she was having engraved. Everything seemed to justify their optimism. James, Marquis of Hamilton, had also joined the fight in the cause of the "royal daughter of Scotland his fair and injured compatriot and relative." Others were coming as well.

On his way Frederick visited Leyden. There he heard Charles Louis and Rupert answering questions for the college examinations. They were both taller than Frederick now and eager to join in the fighting. Ruper particularly urged his father to allow him to come to the front. Frederick however spoke of their obligations to their mother and set off without them. He was by no means the only German prince to be supporting Gustavus Adolphus. The Landgrave of Hesse, the Duke of Lüneburg, even George William, Elector of Brandenburg and the Duke of Saxony were with him. None, however, were as wholehearted in their support as Frederick.

"I only labour for you. Your liberty, which was encroached upon, is the only motive of my coming," Gustavus Adolphus had assured the German Protestants. Most of them were not so sure. Rumour had it that the "Lion of the North" had an eye towards the Imperial seat and a longing to remould the languishing Hapsburg Empire into a Swedish satellite with himself as Emperor. Ferdinand, when he had heard these rumours, had recalled Wallenstein, whom he had dismissed in 1630. His wariness of Wallenstein's aspirations had been superseded by his fear of Gustavus Adolphus, who was now marching through northern Germany with almost as much ease as a trading caravan.

It was in this atmosphere that Frederick, with hardly any clothes, but copious baggage wagons (to enhance his morale), arrived at Frankfort to join Gustavus. The journey had been unpleasant and certainly injurious to his precarious state of health, but his reception seemed to the frayed mind of Frederick like a dream. Gustavus scrupulously addressed him as king, insisted that at table Frederick should take precedence over him and reviled anyone who dared dispute Frederick's rank. At first Frederick basked in his new-found esteem, but gradually there dawned a suspicion that the Swedish King was too servile to be sincere.

On 31 December 1631 Gustavus Adolphus had declared in a letter that "unless our co-religionists in Germany, and particularly the King of Bohemia, be restored to the Palatinate, we cannot see how a secure peace is to be obtained." But when he saw Frederick, prematurely old, uncompromising, melancholy, ailing and impulsive, he wavered. The Palatinate needed a strong ruler who would act as a bulwark against the Catholics. Little knowing what the Swedish King was thinking, Frederick wrote optimistically to the English ambassador, Sir Henry Vane, "I do not press my claim upon his notice at present since, I am confident that all will be well in the end." But the more time Gustavus spent in Frederick's company the more disillusioned he became—much as he tried to disguise his feelings. Frederick in control of the Palatinate would, he felt, be a hindrance rather than a help. Richelieu said as much as well.

Blissfully unaware of the harm he was doing to his cause, Frederick came with the army to Nuremburg where he and Gustavus were given a lavish welcome. From Nuremburg they went to Munich, capital of the hated Maximilian of Bavaria who had seized his Palatine lands and electoral dignity. Frederick in a misguided moment urged Gustavus Adolphus to burn the electoral palace. "Would you have me," was the prudent and much publicised reply, "imitate the Goths, my ancestors, and make my memory as odious as they have rendered theirs?" Gustavus Adolphus' mind was made up. He would offer Frederick terms to be restored to the Palatinate, but only as a Swedish vassal. Frederick defiantly refused. The Lion of the North then petuantly announced that he would not consider allowing Frederick an independent army.

All this Frederick meticulously relayed to Elizabeth in letters or through envoys. Hoping to divert him from his grievances, she replied with letters mostly about domestic matters. Monsieur de Plessen, tutor to the young princes had died. Their eldest daughter, Elizabeth or "La Grecque" as she was called in the nursery because of her statuesque, not quite beautiful, appearance and her love of everything Greek, was now fifteen. Could Frederick apply his mind to finding a husband for her? King Charles had renounced his rights to their grandmother's jewelry in favour of Elizabeth, she enclosed the money for Frederick's use. He promptly returned it saying, "Let it be put out of use, and with the income pay your debts by instalments. I desire nothing of you but that you love me always as much as I love you. No absence, you may well be assured, can chill my love for you, which is very perfect." Elizabeth wrote to him praising the horse Lord Carnarvon had given him. She longed to see Frederick riding again at Rhenen. To pass the time, she tried to involve herself completely in administration, promoting good relations between various ambassadors, calming everyone down when there were quarrels. Sir Henry Vane, for instance, had managed to offend, not only Frederick, but also Gustavus Adolphus. "I did hear of the mal-entendu that passed between the King of Sweden and you, which I was sorry for," Elizabeth was writing in July. "I am glad that all is well again. I know that he himself was sorry for it after that his choler had passed. It is a great pity that he is so subject to that, he hath so many good parts. I pray make the best of all, and remember his good actions and forget his words."

In the meantime the Swedish King and Frederick had parted company. New terms had been offered to Frederick in exchange for part of the Palatinate, but they involved giving the Lutherans religious and educational autonomy. Frederick, as a fervent Calvinist, refused these terms. Disappointed, he left Gustavus believing that the thirty-seven-year-old Scandinavian had no more in common with him than an ability to play tennis.

He set out on his travels again and met his brother's wife for the first time. She was, he reported to Elizabeth, pleasant, but plain. He did not tell her that he looked so ill that Louis had failed to recognise him. His next destination was Heidelberg. There he found that the Spanish were busy burning the castle, taking particular care to smash Elizabeth's beloved Hall of Glass. "These slaughterings and burnings please me not," he wrote miserably. As Frederick moved through Germany he passed the corpses of starving peasants, their mouths stuffed with grass as evidence of a last futile effort to gain nourishment. He heard stories of soldiers whose afternoon occupation might be to line up as many civilians as they could find and see how many could be killed by the same bullet. Everywhere there were signs of devastation. Even his religion, so comforting in its conviction that everything had been predestined and that nothing had been his fault, did not convince him any longer. With each summer had come new hope, but nothing had been achieved and now yet again winter was drawing in. It was the end of the fighting season. As usual Frederick missed the decisive battle of the campaign. It took place at Lützen on 16 November 1632, and was a victory for the Protestants.

Towards the end of the battle a mist had come over the field. One man had become parted from his army and had accidentally, hampered by his short-sightedness, ridden behind the enemy lines. Shot by some plundering soldiers, he was asked, as he was dying, who he was. He replied tersely, "I was the King of Sweden and seal with my blood the liberty and religion of the German people."

Had Frederick heard that Gustavus Adolphus was dead a year or six months before, it might justifiably have been said that it was the news of that which killed him. As it was he had lost faith in the new Augustus and it was his own weakly physique, totally exhausted by the endless campaigns and disappointments of the last twelve years that finally released him. He caught the plague at Bacharach, the place which nineteen years before had been chosen as a dividing line between the financial responsibilities of the "most learned King of Christendom" and the promising young Elector Palatine on his wedding journey. Then he had avoided Bacharach because of an outbreak of the plague. Now he had finally come there, and succumbed, almost like a death wish, to the terrible disease which his weary consumptive body could not shake off. His last thoughts were of the young girl whom he had once escorted to Heidelberg. "As to himself," he said, "she would only lose one whose chief merit had been that she had constantly been the dearest object of his existence."

CHAPTER ELEVEN

"Though Dr Rumpf told it me very discreetly it was the first time that I ever was frighted," Elizabeth said much later. Nothing could have been more unexpected than the news which reached her on that cold November morning. Only two weeks before Frederick had written to her: "Do not put yourself in pain; there is no danger to be feared for me here." Of course she had believed him.

Now there seemed to be nothing to hope for. Gone was the comforting prospect of an idyllic life alone with Frederick in Rhenen or Heidelberg or Prague. There was also, she realised rather to her surprise, nothing more to be afraid of. Nothing could touch her now. She was stunned at first. "It seemed to take away my faculties, although not my sense of misery," she commented later. For three days she said nothing. She could not sleep, eat or cry. People who were not afraid for her life, wondered about her sanity.

While Elizabeth struggled with her grief, the precincts of the Wassaenor Hof had become alive with rumours. King Charles in England had smallpox, perhaps he would die. The shock of that following so quickly on the death of Frederick would certainly kill the Queen of Bohemia. There was talk that the King of Sweden was still alive. The implications of Frederick's death were widely discussed. A Mr Parry wrote to Lord Brooke: "If the King of Bohemia be dead, the Emperor hath a great advantage thereby, because there is none now living but himself that hath any title to that so long controverted crown. Besides upon that King's death, our King and State are obliged to do more for a nephew than for a brother-in-law, and more likewise for a widow than for a wife."

By then the "widow" had emerged from her room and had begun to wander among the faded tapestries, bitten, one of her daughters later observed, by successive generations of rats and mice, and then into the gardens with the clipped hedges and geometrical paths. Every step was observed. She looked older, was the general consensus of opinion. A certain vibrance had gone. Or was it merely the effect of transient grief? "The Queen," wrote one of her ladies-in-waiting, "takes this affliction very heavily, but not extravagantly and grieves so inwardly to herself as I fear she will hardly overcome it."

But somehow Elizabeth did overcome it. She had her rooms draped conventionally in black and she began writing letters which were strangely diffident in tone, less ebullient, less daring and more restrained. "There never lived a better husband nor more careful than he was of me," she wrote sadly, "and daily more and more I find his loss. I shall ever grieve for him so long as I live for the contentment I had in the work was in him and it is dead with him."

On her writing desk she found a letter from her brother written in his own hand:

My dearest and only sister, Never did I rail at any opportunity for writing to you excepting this one—and although I do not wish my hand to be so unfortunate as even to name it, yet I will not have the vanity to imagine that I can be a few lines, efface the just grief which this last misfortune has brought upon you; but still I would hereby express the love and service which I owe you on this occasion (knowing that good friends are best proved in the greatest adversities) and I know not how you can just now reap as much fruit from, or have as true a knowledge of my efforts to serve you, as in coming to be with me. Therefore, my dearest sister, I entreat you to make as much haste as you conveniently can to come to me, where I doubt not but you will find some little comfort for your own sadness, as you will greatly relieve that of him who is, in life or death

My dearest sister,
Your most affectionate brother to serve you,
Charles.

The smallpox had been very mild. Charles had quite forgotten himself as he wrote that letter. All the old love and affection had revived. He was now, with Frederick's brother, Prince Louis Palatine, the guardian of his sister's children, her protector. Unlike King James, King Charles accepted the risks of having Elizabeth in England. She might be the heroine of the Puritans, albeit unwillingly, but she was also his sister. Besides he had never been calculating. He had always allowed himself to be swayed by his feelings in a way that his father had never done. But Elizabeth did not accept his invitation. She wrote to him instead entreating "you to pardon me, if I cannot at present obey your command and my own wishes; the custom in Germany being not to stir out of the house for some time, after such a misfortune. And since I was married into this country, I should wish to observe its customs carefully."

Moreover she had to consider her children. If she went to England she would in effect be abandoning their cause. That she would never do. By now she had decided that she would exist entirely for them. It was not altogether an easy decision. Elizabeth had never been very maternal. Perhaps the shock of her unexpected first pregnancy when she was only seventeen had affected her. Certainly she had been too adventurous and too intelligent for the responsibilities of motherhood to have come so early. She always tended to view her daughters, at least, as rivals rather than as members of a different generation and she made no secret of the fact that she preferred her sons. But even among them only Charles Louis had really been wanted.

Her children, however, were perhaps the most remarkable facet of her life. All of them were exceptional and at least four of them had something of genius about them. Perversely it was the least likeable on whom Elizabeth doted. Charles Louis had grown into a priggish, self-centred and insincere young man. In appearance he was still fair, with pretensions to good looks. He was not affectionate, nor was he particularly good at anything, although he did have a pronounced aptitude, which he shared with his youngest sister, for making cruelly caustic remarks. But he was brave and, like all Elizabeth's children, he was rather precocious. He also understood the essence of charm. After the birth of Frederick Henry, followed by a gap of four years, Elizabeth had begun to yearn for another child if only to dispel those rumours that she and Frederick were unlikely to have any more children. Charles Louis had been welcome. She had even taken waters to improve her health before his birth. Now she was proud that he was "hasting to the field" to join the Stathouder's army. "I think he cannot too soon be a soldier in this active time," she announced. He was sixteen. It was a pity, she felt, that, while Charles Louis was learning to be a soldier, sho would be deprived of his company and forced to rely on the companionship of her eldest daughter instead.

La Grecque was also the child of her mother's untroubled youth. "She knew every language and science under the sun," her youngest sister recorded. But mother and daughter were incompatible. They never learned to understand each other. Where the elder Elizabeth loved taking exercise and could imagine nothing more fulfilling than following the hounds at the hunt, the young Elizabeth would delight in poring over chemical experiments with her brother Rupert and would deride sport as frivolous. Often she would irritate her mother by being "very absent", immersed in the history of Greece and ancient languages. She disliked music and never managed to paint competently. Moreover she did not succeed in being beautiful. That was a puzzle, because she had all the ingredients of great beauty: a flawless complexion, good bone structure, dark hair, "brown sparkling eyes, a well-shaped forehead, beautiful cherry lips and a sharp aquiline nose", her sister Sophia recalled. But the nose did have a habit of turning bright red just when something important was happening and her eyes were slightly too round, contributing something rather prim and precise to her appearance, which deprived it of the perfection and appeal it would otherwise have had.

After Charles Louis, Elizabeth loved Rupert best. The child who had nearly been forgotten in Prague seemed made for adventure. He was robust. "Bodily health," wrote Sophia later, "is an inheritance from our mother which no-one can dispute with me, the best we ever had from her of which Rupert hath taken a double share." He was also charming, good-looking, witty, abominably rude to his sisters, and slightly uncouth. He was a brilliant amateur. "A little giddy", was how his mother described him. The truth was that she never could control him. She tried, of course, but whatever fetters she created he would always manage to free himself and do just as he wished without appearing at all disobedient.

Maurice was a weaker version of Rupert and, as his mother had anticipated at his birth, he seemed born for the battlefield. He was slapdash, athletic and brave.

Louise, the second daughter, was very like Rupert. She painted and (according to her sister and the evidence that remains) "her talent for it was so strong that she would take likenesses without seeing the originals." She was Gerard Honthorst's prize pupil, but there is just a hint of mockery, almost cruelty, in her pictures which makes one wonder why people on the whole liked her without reservation. But they did, and neither the fact that she did not care how she dressed nor the fact that she always retained a certain childish impetuosity ever diminished a general feeling of respect for her.

Of the boys, Edward was the most strikingly good-looking. He was well-intentioned, but rather empty-headed. Like all Elizabeth's children, he was a brilliant linguist, reading with equal ease the works of Shakespeare and the Heidelberg Catechism.

Henrietta was still only six. Her "fair flaxen hair and complexion without exaggeration of lilies and roses" were reminiscent of her grandmother, Anne of Denmark, when she had been young. According to her sister Sophia, "she had soft eyes, black well-arched eyebrows, an admirable contour of face and forehead, a pretty mouth, and hands and arms as perfect as if they had been turned on a lathe." She was certainly going to be beautiful, but even now there was something too ethereal and too delicate about her.

Philip, who shortly after his father's death had spurred his mother on by asking, "Is the battle lost then, because the King is dead?" was the second youngest son. He already showed signs of acute sensitivity and impetuosity.

Sophia was, as yet, hardly able to crawl across the floor at Leyden. She was the one who would record the characters and actions of her brothers and sisters and eventually found the Hanoverian line. Already she was a keen observer and threatened to be a brilliant mimic. She had a way of constantly demanding attention and getting it. She was practical, quick at learning, witty, nearly beautiful but not quite, and sensitive.

The last child, Gustavus, showed ominous signs of being an epileptic.

All these children were educated along strictly German lines. Sophia later gave an account of their upbringing. "At Leyden," she wrote, "we had a court quite in the German style. Our house as well as our curtsies were all laid down by rule. My governess, whose name was Madame de Ples had held the same post with my father when he was a child and from this fact her probable age may be guessed. She was, however, assisted in her duties by two daughters, who looked older than their mother. Their conduct was equally upright towards God and man. I believe that they prayed to God and never disturbed man, for their appearance was frightful enough to terrify little children. . . .

"I rose at seven in the morning, and was obliged to go every day *en déshabillé* to Mademoiselle Marie de Quat, one of the ladies before mentioned, who made me pray and read the Bible. She then set me to learn the *Quadrains de Pibrac*, while she employed the time in brushing her teeth; her grimaces during the performance are more firmly fixed in my memory than the lessons which she tried to teach. I was then dressed and prepared by half-past eight to endure the regular succession of teacher after teacher.

"They kept me busy until ten o'clock, except when, to my comfort, kind Providence sent them a cold in the head. At ten o'clock the dancing-master was always welcome, for he gave me exercise till eleven, which was the dinner hour. This meal always took place with great ceremony at a long table. On entering the dining room I found all my brothers drawn up in front, with their governors and gentlemen posted behind in the same order side by side. I was obliged by rule to make first a very low curtsy to the princes, a slighter one to the others, another low one on placing myself opposite to them, then another slight one to my governess, who on entering the room with her daughters curtsied very low to me. I was obliged to curtsy again on handing over my gloves to their custody, then again on placing myself opposite to my brothers, again when the gentlemen brought me a large basin in which to wash my hands, again after grace was said, and for the last and ninth time on seating myself at table.

"Everything was so arranged that we knew on each day of the week what we were to eat, as is the case in convents. On Sundays and Wednesdays two divines and two professors were always invited to dine with us. . . . After dinner I rested till two o'clock, when my teachers returned to the charge. At six I supped, and at half-past eight went to bed, having said my prayers and read some chapters of the Bible."

And so it was, never altering year in and year out with only one ambition—release from the routine as soon as possible. Nevertheless it instilled into them all a feeling of security which, despite their precarious worldly position, never deserted them. It also equipped them perfectly to occupy a place in the world which would never be theirs.

By 1633 two of "those unfortunate children," as Elizabeth described her brilliant brood, had come to live with her in the Hague. They were La Grecque and Louise. Two more, Charles Louis and Rupert, went to fight in the Stathouder's army against the Spanish. It had been easy enough to let them go, but no sooner had they left than Elizabeth heard disquieting reports about the immoralities of camp life. She hurriedly despatched a message that Rupert must return home. A child who was "a little giddy" might easily be corrupted. He came, somewhat reluctantly, but soon the Stathouder had given Elizabeth such firm assurances about his welfare that she had to release him again.

Left with her two eldest daughters and the uneventfulness of the Hague, Elizabeth decided that the time had come for her to set to work on behalf of her eldest son. She did so with as much dedication as she had always given to Frederick's affairs. She rid herself of the conventional mourning clothes and in their place she wore either plain white or plain black trimmed with lace. As usual the neckline was a little lower than fashion dictated, but trifles of that sort, which had never really bothered her, ceased to matter at all now. It was her work that concerned her and she would have been lost without that.

At first there were the usual financial worries, and these persisted despite the equivalent of approximately £140,000 a year (in today's money) which Elizabeth was receiving from King Charles. Then there was a possibility that Louis Palatine might not accept the duties of Administrator until Charles Louis' majority, and that the Catholic Duke of Neuberg might take them on instead. Frederick's young brother, who was happily married, had been wary of involving himself in the problems which had virtually killed Frederick, but his mother managed to persuade him where his duties lay and from then on he did his best to carry them out.

Elizabeth then arranged to send a representative to the Protestant Princes' meeting at Heilbrunn and instructed him to tell the meeting that no solution would be acceptable to her unless it constituted the complete restitution of the Palatinate to Charles Louis. The result of the meeting was that Sweden agreed to hand over the Palatinate to the representatives of Charles Louis as long as it was adequately defended and 6,000 rix dollars were paid towards the expenses. Louis Palatine generously promised to raise half the money, but raising the other half ultimately proved an insurmountable problem. It was quite impossible to expect anything from the indigenous population of the Palatinate and it was unrealistic to hope for much from King Charles. Sympathetic though he might be, he dared not recall Parliament who alone could release the money.

Elizabeth sent the loquacious, but well-intentioned, Sir Francis Nethersole, to plead with her brother. It was a mistake. Sir Francis was loyal to Elizabeth, but he was neither an orator nor a diplomat. King Charles, remote, introverted, and cursed with a strange falsetto voice, was difficult enough for a stranger to get on with. Nethersole did not try. He disliked King Charles. He was convinced that he had treated Elizabeth badly and he said so. He reproached the aloof and insecure King for hampering the Palatines' cause and he disrupted a plan to raise the money through voluntary contributions. King Charles was incensed with Nethersole and eventually ordered that he should be arrested. Somehow as this order was being carried out the secretary escaped and found temporary sanctuary in the house of the Dutch Ambassador where he wrote a letter to Elizabeth. He then gave himself up and was lodged in the Tower.

The whole matter was not conducive to Elizabeth's peace of mind. She had confided some state secrets in Nethersole and her letters had been rather too outspoken. She was horrified when she learnt that the Council were reading them and that their contents had been relayed to her brother. In one she had expressed her despair of success in England and her fear that she might be forced to seek the help of France. But it was the humiliation that really hurt. "As for my brother," she wrote indignantly to Lord Arundel, "if he at any time should have desire to have seen what I writ to Nethersole, or what private commands I did give him, I was very willing he should see all." The affair dragged on for months. Nethersole could not keep quiet. When the Book of Common Prayer was reprinted referring to Elizabeth merely as Princess, he was garrulously indignant. Elizabeth did her best to calm him down, and she remained loyal to him. The result was that a rift developed between her and her brother. It was never entirely repaired.

Richelieu in France tried to exploit the situation. Hercule de Charnacé, the French Ambassador, pestered Elizabeth to desert her brother and accept the protection of the French. Elizabeth would not do so, whatever she may have told Nethersole. "I fear the physician as much as the disease," she declared, "for though the French have succoured Heidelberg, yet I cannot trust them as long as they call not my brother-in-law administrator, nor my son elector."

Nevertheless King Charles continued to suspect that his sister might eventually turn to France. It was more through fear than love that he kept in touch with her now. He presented Charles Louis with the Order of the Garter as a gesture of goodwill and, when his son James was born in October 1633, he invited Elizabeth and Charles Louis and the Prince of Orange to be god-parents. Elizabeth, in her turn, encouraged her children to correspond with their uncle just as she had once invoked Frederick Henry to write to his grandfather. The result was a continuous amicable correspondence between Whitehall and the Hague. On one occasion Rupert wrote declaring that he desired "nothing more than to grow up for your Majesties service". But compliments, however genuine, would never persuade King Charles to finance an army for Charles Louis to lead into the Palatinate. Instead, as a gesture of goodwill, he sent an ambassador to Denmark to secure Elizabeth's inheritance from her maternal grandmother.

Charles Louis was disappointed. He longed to gain his spurs and he seldom spoke of anything but his proposed march into Germany. To the English however the French threat still remained. They would sooner do nothing than virtually issue an invitation to the French to fraternise with Charles Louis by financing an army. Anyway they knew Charles Louis would not be as welcome in Germany as he anticipated.

In 1634 Elizabeth sent Rusdorf to her dower at Franckenthal to help the residents. She also instructed him to store some grain in case of seige and to send her some Rhenish wine. The report that Rusdorf sent back was depressing: "The people are outraged and impoverished," he wrote, "the country is in no wise cultivated, but trodden down by troops, the master and his ministers without authority, the granaries and cellars empty, commerce annihilated, coffers exhausted." More important Elizabeth had wanted Rusdorf to find at last a suitable burial place for Frederick. Even death had not brought him peace. The Rhinelanders had pelted his coffin with mud on its way to Franckenthal. Now with the enemy drawing nearer he must continue his wearisome journey. Louis, his brother, and Rusdorf tried to have him buried in Sedan, but this was French territory and the French raised objections. In the end no record was kept of his burial place. The loyal Rusdorf escorted his master on his last journey, finally coming to Metz and presumably burying him privately there.

It was now that the "most resplendent Queen, even in the darkness of fortune," as Henry Wotton described her, began to fall ill. In July 1635 she wrote to Sir Thomas Roe assuring him that she had "got up [her] strength again" after an "ague" which lasted eight weeks, during which she had suffered twenty-nine fits. She was nearly forty and everything indicated that the best was past. Her looks, her aura of radiance, even her vivacity had waned and, where she had once quested after excitement, she now dedicated herself to the less exhilarating exigencies of duty. Her own importance had diminished with the birth of direct heirs to her brother and it was now around her children that her machinations revolved. It was not enough. It was unlikely that someone who had commanded so much attention in the past could easily devote herself to other people. She grew envious of her daughters and jealous of their admirers. It was with a certain, but definite, unease that she realised that the young Frederick William of Brandenburg had been recalled home, not because his studies at Leyden were completed, nor because he was needed at home, but because he had fallen in love with her wilfully beautiful daughter Louise.

But it was really her sons who concerned her. Most of her plans hinged on Charles Louis. She was determined now that he should visit England. Perhaps the proximity of his nephew would stimulate King Charles' conscience and revive old loyalties. She did not negotiate for an invitation. Instead she simply made arrangements for his journey and then wrote announcing that he was on his way. By September John Dinley was writing to Sir Thomas Roe: "many are busy sending the Prince Elector into England." By October he had arrived.

The atmosphere of Whitehall had altered since Elizabeth had been there. Like the Continent it had experienced great changes. The problem of inflation was worse than it had ever been, but some of the dignity of the court had returned and was personified in the languid grandeur of the paintings of Anthony van Dyke. Fashions were more subdued and the women were less made-up than they had been in James I's time. Altogether it was a more suitable place for a young man who had just reached his majority and who was eager to make a name for himself.

Elizabeth had been rather apologetic about Charles Louis. "A very ill courtier", she described him. Nevertheless he was a great success. The young man, his hair still fair and his face not yet marred by an expression of cynicism which was to disfigure it in later years made such a good impression that Elizabeth hurriedly despatched her younger son Rupert to England as well.

They both loved England. How different it was from the dreary provincialism of the Hague. Even the food was better. Tables piled high with mutton, capons, pullets, duck, partridge, artichokes, lamb, pheasant, cherries, veal, salmon, carp and tenches. And not a thought need be given about how the bills would be paid.

But their trip to England did emphasise the disharmony between the two brothers. While Charles Louis became deeply embroiled in political intrigue on his own account and even involved himself with the Puritan fringe, Rupert threw himself into a life of ceaseless pleasure. It was after all his first opportunity and he took it with a zest that pleased his uncle. "His Majesty," Thomas Roe informed Elizabeth, "takes great pleasure in his [Rupert's] unrestfulness, for he is never idle; in his sports serious, in his conversation retired, but sharp and witty when occasion provokes him."

Charles Louis was envious of his younger brother's success. While he, "so sensible of his own affairs", collected funds for the Palatinate, Rupert spent his time in apparent idleness perhaps even admiring what Charles Louis' new friends termed the "old rotten pictures" in King Charles' collection. It was all too frivolous and Charles Louis determined to put a stop to it. With typical churlishness he wrote to his mother hinting darkly that Rupert might be on the verge of becoming a Catholic and was spending far too much time "with the Queen and her ladies and her Papists." Rupert, he also reported, had become a friend of the half-Spanish Endymion Porter, who, as long ago as 1622, had, according to rumour, made some disparaging remarks about Elizabeth. Charles Louis could not deny however that his brother was perfectly agreeable when they met. Whatever his faults, and whatever "windmills," as his mother termed them, might be reeling in his mind, Rupert was always scrupulously polite.

The present windmill was enormous. A plan had been instigated by King Charles to send Prince Rupert to Madagascar to colonise and rule it. It was the third largest island in the world and might prove a stepping stone towards India. To keep Charles Louis happy, King Charles had offered him the governorship of the West Indies. Charles Louis and Rupert were both enthusiastic and they wrote to their mother imploring her to support the scheme. Horrified, she announced that she wanted "none of her sons to be knights-errant" and anyway, she pointed out, "if Madagascar"—for of course it was quite out of the question that Charles Louis could be governing anywhere but the Palatinate—"if the place was either worth the taking or possible to be kept, the Portuguese by this time would have it, having so long possessed the coast of Africa near it." How, she wondered, could the arrangements have gone so far without her knowledge? Already Sir William Davenant, and in his wake some less competent poets, had written ballads about the scheme and these had been distributed throughout London. History it seemed was repeating itself. With what certainty had she set off to Bohemia all those years ago ignoring what she knew would be her father's advice. How much she sympathised with Rupert's longing for adventure and how much she feared for him. "A most desperate, dangerous, unwholesome, fruitless action," was how Sir Thomas Roe saw it. Elizabeth, sharing his view wholeheartedly, wrote to Rupert imploring him to desist from such a venture. Rupert, who was already studying navigation, ship-building and mineralogy in preparation for his journey, obeyed his mother grudgingly. The disappointment soon gave way to a feeling of restlessness and dissatisfaction.

Charles Louis did not feel as frustrated by his loss of the proposed governorship of the West Indies. More cautious than Rupert, he had only ever half believed that it would all be as easy as it sounded. He too remembered the catastrophes of Heidelberg and Bohemia. Besides he had family responsibilities and he was beginning to feel that he was not being treated with the respect he deserved. In July 1636 he was writing to his mother: "I think it something strange, that I may have no copy of anything concerning my own business, which was never denied to the King my father. I see no reason why the King should mistrust it in my hand, considering that, for my own sake, I must keep it secret." He was also on the defensive. "I sent you by him," he continued, "a measure of my true height without any heels. I believe your Majesty sent for it, because they think my brother Maurice as high as myself."

He began to assert himself in small but irritating ways. Why, he demanded of his mother, had someone not been reprimanded for boxing Louise' ears in public? Had the Palatines lost their dignity? Moreover he observed that it was time his eldest sister married. He distrusted all the studying she indulged in encouraged by her friend Anna Maria van Schurman. That girl spoke six languages, besides her own, excelled in painting, carving, knowledge of the arts, theology, philosophy, science, astronomy and many other accomplishments. Elizabeth would be better occupied, he felt, hunting, as her mother did, for venison. That at least could feed the family. As it was she was merely another mouth to feed with money which, in his view, would be better spent on his campaign. Unfortunately, there were not many suitors for a princess who, although she purported to be beautiful, was far too well-read for a woman, had no money and almost as little political significance.

When the King of Poland offered for her, Charles Louis was therefore delighted. Never mind that he was already twice-married and middle-aged. His mother was less callous. She advised caution. For a start she was offended because the proposal had been made to King Charles instead of to her. Charles Louis did his best to reassure her on this point. The reason, he explained, rather lamely, why the Roman Catholic King of Poland "treated of no particulars with your Majesty . . . [was] . . . because he hopeth the King will not look so strictly to the religion as your Majesty." However there were more practical problems that concerned Elizabeth. Poland was the traditional enemy of Sweden. Might not the Palatines' ally take "umbrage" or feel "discontent" at the match? The Queen of Bohemia also pointed out that Poland was an "Elective Kingdom," and any children of the match would have no guarantee of support. Above all, she could not agree to her daughter changing her religion. Nothing would persuade her to accede to such a condition. "If it be found good for my son's affairs," she decided, "and there be good conditions for religion", she would not prevent it.

But it was not only from the Queen of Bohemia's point of view that the situation was a tricky one. However much the King of Poland longed to be married to the intelligent rather beautiful young Elizabeth, and even though he did wear "her picture publicly" according to Sir Thomas Roe, it was not going to be easy for him to welcome her into his country. He seemed to prefer Protestant princesses and this had not gone unobserved by his intensely conservative Roman Catholic countrymen. There had been Mary Eleanor of Brandenburg whom he had been thwarted from marrying and now people recalled that as a child he had had an "heretical nurse". Perhaps that explained it. The Poles were wary. Wladislaus approached the Pope for a dispensation, but it was not really the Pope he needed to persuade. At the Diet of Warsaw the whole matter was discussed among the Poles. Wladislaus's tears failed to move them and they refused to accept a Protestant queen. Their King was not prepared to surrender his throne for Elizabeth and she did not consider him worth a mass. And so the match came to nothing. He returned to his mistresses, she to her books, and King Charles wrote to his sister, "He is unworthy of either of our thoughts, except it be to make him smart for his base dealing with us." Very soon after this the Polish King declared himself an ally of the Emperor.

By then the Palatines' fortunes had never seemed at a lower ebb. The murder of the Imperialist general Wallenstein by the Emperor's own men had made little difference. The focus of the war's activity was now the conference table rather than the battlefield. In 1635 the Peace of Prague had been signed committing the troops of Maximilian of Bavaria and those of John George of Saxony to fight under the Imperial flag. Maximilian, ageing and thoroughly confused by the vicissitudes in his fortunes over the last twenty years, married the Emperor's daughter, who was forty years younger than he was. He hoped for an heir and accordingly he was confirmed as the Elector and his title made hereditary. Other German princes signed the treaty and these included, much to the disgust of Louisa Juliana, the Elector of Brandenburg. Only Charles Louis, the Landgrave of Hesse-Cassel and the Duke of Brunswick-Lüneburg stood outside the treaty, alienated from Vienna. Under the treaty there were provisions for toleration towards Lutheranism, but still no recognition of Calvinism. It was evident however that the war no longer revolved around religion and it was the fact that the Swedes had gained nothing from their intervention in Germany and that France now declared war against Spain that ensured that the devastation of Germany was not over. The treaty simply heralded a pause, which was hardly noticeable, while the various combatants took stock of their situation.

Beyond the boundaries of Germany, Denmark seemed to favour the Emperor; England did nothing; the Netherlands was divided among its own people; the Swedish troops were on the brink of mutiny. The French army, which now joined in the war, was weaker than was generally believed and disintegrated after an initial victory. The Spanish were repulsed from the gates of Paris.

But, as the fighting escalated again, it was the people of the Palatinate and the rest of Germany who were the sufferers. Their agony went on, regardless of treaties, regardless of the present imbalance on the European stage. Starvation, brutality and disease were rife. "From Coln hither," one observer remarked, "all the towns, villages and castles be battered, pillaged and burnt." People lay starving in the streets, cannibalism was frequently reported and the sole ambition of most of the inhabitants was to find something to eat whether it was horse-meat, acorns, grass, cats or dogs. Germany, stumbling on the brink of civilisation, had been tossed back into the dark ages.

In February 1637 the Emperor Ferdinand, asthmatic and prematurely old at 59, died. He was confident that he had achieved most of what he had hoped for and that he could go to his maker in peace. Austria was no longer the sick old lady of Europe. The Roman Catholics remained in charge. Moreover he had left an heir and the succession was secure. Ferdinand III however was very different from his father. He was weaker and less convinced in the absolute rightness of his cause. This was enough to give a subtle shift to the balance of power.

It was to this Europe that Charles Louis and Rupert returned in June. It was easy for Charles Louis to leave England. He had managed to obtain the loan of a fleet from King Charles and the promise of £10,000 from Lord Craven. The young Elector longed to go to the Palatinate, which was now yet again in the hands of the enemy, and regain his territories in one swift campaign. But for Rupert it was different. The future seemed to hold very little for him. He began his last morning out hunting with King Charles by announcing that he hoped he would break his neck so that he could leave his bones in England.

Nothing untoward did happen, however, and Rupert and Charles Louis set sail for Holland. They found their mother worn out by two years of continuous quarrelling among various factions of her court and with her servants. She was depressed because her house and furniture were now so shabby that she had to see some of the visitors to the Hague in the gardens of the Binnenhof, although it was so hot that summer that it was really the best place to meet. And then even her principles had had to be compromised. Charming though her real friends were, she was beginning to realise that they had little influence over her brother. She disliked Archbishop Laud, with whom in the past she had exchanged nothing more than an occasional "cold compliment", but with whom she had now been advised to make a friend on account of his influence with the King. Elizabeth therefore embarked on a correspondence which was a chore rather than a pleasure. She considered the Archbishop unpractical and stupid and his ideas she felt were irritating and sometimes naive. She was not entirely without justification. On being asked what ought to be done with Rupert, Laud had suggested that he should be made a bishop. Moreover he had an unrealistic faith in treaties. "I confess as a woman and a Christian," Elizabeth wrote to him on this point, "I should rather desire it [the restitution] by peace, but I have lived so long amongst soldiers and wars, as it makes one to me as easy as the other and as familiar, especially when I remember never to have read in the chronicles of my ancestors, that any king of England got any good by treaties, but most commonly lost by them, and on the contrary, by wars made always good peaces."

When her two sons arrived home it was to find their mother looking older. She in her turn noticed that Charles Louis had grown a moustache and had acquired a more cynical air. But somehow everything about him pleased her and she was delighted to hear from the gouty Sir Thomas Roe that her eldest son had left behind him in England "such an odour of his sweetness and virtues that all men mourn his departure." She was not so happy about Rupert. She found his flippancy disconcerting and he was still, she decided, rather too headstrong. She could not agree with Roe's assessment of him: "Whatsoever he [Rupert] undertakes he does it vigorously and seriously." It was a pity, in her view, that he did not undertake more. He had refused to fall in with a plan to marry the rather plain daughter of the extremely wealthy leader of the French Protestants and so at least finance his family until their situation improved. Nevertheless he was always eager to fight. Now he wanted to join his brother, Maurice, in the Prince of Orange's army in the besieged town of Breda. Elizabeth let him go.

The venture was a success. Reports reached her that Rupert and Maurice had infiltrated behind the enemy lines, discovered when the Spanish were going to attack and warned the Prince of Orange's troops. They had followed this up by fighting bravely throughout the ensuing engagement. The two boys had actually enjoyed the fighting and even the corpses of their friends lying at their feet hardly seemed to deter them.

For Elizabeth the victorious outcome was marred by the death of the Landgrave of Hesse-Cassel, a relation of Frederick's, who had always been loyal to the Palatines' cause. He left an army which Elizabeth, no sooner had she recovered from her grief, tried to secure for Charles Louis. However, to her chagrin, it was Bernard of Saxe-Weimar who took it over.

Charles Louis was therefore left at the end of another fighting season with nothing more than energy and good intentions. Indeed all his thoughts were devoted to his one aim: regaining the Palatinate. His continual preoccupation with this guaranteed that winter in the Hague would be as gloomy as ever. Elizabeth's health was poor and she quarrelled continuously with her daughters. They, in their turn, regretted the fact that they had so few dresses and, whenever they went out, were compelled, for reasons of frugality, to walk rather than drive in a coach. There was only one colourful interlude before campaigning began again. The young sister of the Princess of Orange was marrying Baron de Brederode and, because the girl was one of Elizabeth's ladies-in-waiting, Elizabeth made it an excuse for having a celebration. Naturally that involved tilting, in which, on this occasion, Charles Louis and Rupert both excelled. They rode on white horses in mediaeval costume. Watching them revived some of Elizabeth's former gaiety, so that by the time supper had been eaten and the ball which followed it had commenced she had completely forgotten the pressures of the present. She decided that during the weeks that followed there must be more tilting matches. These continued until Elizabeth retired to Rhenen for the summer.

She preferred Rhenen to the Hague. Her children came to visit her and she actually enjoyed their company as they chattered among each other in French, sometimes breaking their conversation to make some comment in English to their mother. How different it was here. The house she and Frederick had planned together dominated the little town with its tower and river and marshy fields. Nothing seemed to annoy and depress her, as she looked out of the windows to the Lombardy poplars in the west and the wooded hills to the east.

But no sooner had Elizabeth settled down at Rhenen than invariably something happened which made it imperative that she should return to the Hague. This year it was the visit of Marie de Medici, mother of Henrietta Maria, who, despite King Charles' protests, was on her way to England. "I came here from Rhenen," Elizabeth wrote to Sir Thomas Roe in August 1638, "to receive Queen-mother. Her coming hither will make you not a little wonder. She doth use me very kindly, but keeps her greatness enough, for she kissed none but me."

Marie de Medici, with whom Elizabeth was compelled to spend a lot of time, was not someone likely to appeal to her. Like Elizabeth, the mother of Louis XIII was an exile. Chafing under Richelieu's grandeur, she had plotted against the powerful minister and believed she would overthrow him. But the "Day of the Dupes" proved how wrong she was and the last eight years had been spent in exile in Brussels. She was pathetically proud, and made herself unpopular in the Hague, communicating with no-one but the Queen of Bohemia simply because she believed that there was no-one else worth communicating with. It was a great relief to the Dutch when she eventually set sail for England. "Cave only waits for a wind," Elizabeth wrote, "which is yet contrary. I think Queen-mother is cause of it; for she is gone very suddenly from hence, with scarce taking leave, towards England, though Sir William Boswell did all he could to detain her. I think the wind loves our country in keeping her as long as it can out of it."

As Marie of Medicis made her way to England, Elizabeth reflected that nothing but harm would come of the visit. News was constantly reaching her of Charles' problems with his subjects. The disagreeable and rather stupid mother of his wife flanked by Roman Catholics would ignite further political problems and prove another financial liability. For her part, Elizabeth regretted the small dogs she had sent with such care to the Queen Mother in Paris all these years ago.

In the meantime Charles Louis and Rupert had gone into Germany accompanied by Lord Craven, who was spending a large sum of money on the campaign. Charles Louis was obviously straining on the leash his mother had imposed on him. He hated being given advice and the fact that Elizabeth had particularly told him to heed any advice Sir Thomas Roe might give him exacerbated this feeling. It was in vain that Roe explained to him that "the deep contrivings of plots of war are not be be expected from a Prince of twenty years, but in his youth so long as your Highness continues generous, and forward in brave actions your name will not be more honoured amongst your friends, than reproachable among your enemies." He hardly listened. His mother realised this and grew more anxious. Charles Louis was, she felt, "impertinent" and also, ominously, he "has too many correspondences". In fact he was almost outside her control.

Once in Germany he determined on breaking off a wing of the Imperial army and attacking that. There were a few successful skirmishes and then inevitably with the first important battle, came disaster. The Swedes deserted at the crucial moment and Charles Louis was forced to flee. It was an ignominious flight. He lost his coach and horse and his other belongings including his Garter insignia, which his father had also lost during the most desperate flight of his life. Rupert and Lord Craven were less careful of their safety. They fought on. At last they were surrounded by Imperialists and Rupert was hurled to the ground. "I am a colonel," he announced proudly, looking up at his captors with their white ribbons flowing in the breeze and their standards flying. "A very young one," was the reply.

CHAPTER TWELVE

In November 1638 Edward Nicholas wrote to a friend: "We have received sad news of the defeat of the Prince Palatine's army at their first entrance into action. The Palsgrave hardly escaped by swimming over a river, his brother is taken prisoner and since dead of his many wounds, having fought very bravely, and (as the gazette says) like a lion." Elizabeth heard similar reports but nothing definite. The suspense made her ill and, in what she later described as a fit of "passion", she wrote: "If he [Rupert] be prisoner, I confess it would be no small grief to me, for I wish [him] rather dead than in his enemies' [hands]."

In fact Rupert, Lord Craven and Ferentz were safely at Warrendorf in the hands of the Imperialists. If it could be called safety, for they were under the charge of the same Colonel Devereux who had murdered Wallenstein and who would probably be prepared to murder anyone else if he was required to do so. Rupert spent the weeks there trying to engineer an escape, but he achieved nothing more than sending a note to King Charles assuring him that he was alive and well.

Once Elizabeth had been reassured about Rupert's physical safety, she began to worry about his spiritual well-being. Was it possible that he might be converted to the Catholic faith? She was certain that the Imperialists would try to convert him. It would be impossible for their propaganda machine to resist the temptation to exploit a Palatine convert. Lord Craven, who had bought his own release, had failed to purchase Rupert's as well. Selflessly he offered twice as much money to be allowed to share Rupert's prison with him. His offer was rejected, but Elizabeth still hoped to find someone to safeguard her son's religion. "I think if we could send some honest understanding man to him . . . it would be very good for Rupert," she said. It was to no avail and, having tried everything she could in that direction she turned her thoughts to "him I love most".

She grieved at Charles Louis' misfortunes where she had only harped on Rupert's. She was furious when she heard that her cousin the Duke of Brunswick-Lüneburg had sent a thousand men to help the Emperor. "Tun of Beer" she called him heatedly. On the other hand she was delighted that the King of Denmark was giving Charles Louis such a generous welcome at Glückstadt. She hoped it would be followed by some military assistance, for Charles Louis was already planning another campaign. Admittedly it didn't look very promising, but there was always the expectation that something would turn up which would give him some idea where to concentrate his efforts.

It was the death of the Duke of Saxe-Weimar that gave Charles Louis his new sense of direction. His mother urged him to go to England to raise the money and support which would enable him to take over the army. King Charles gave him £25,000 and advised him to consult the French about purchasing the army so as not to offend them. The trouble was that, unknown to the English King, Richelieu wanted the army himself. And so when Charles Louis arrived at Boulogne without a passport, and made his way to Paris with a certain amount of ceremony, he was walking into a trap. Nothing untoward happened until he set off from Paris in disguise and incognito. This gave Richelieu the opportunity he had been waiting for. He pretended to interpret Charles Louis' journey as being underhand and when the young Elector reached Moulins on 24 October 1639, he was arrested and not very ceremoniously conducted to the prison of Vincennes. Three of his brothers, Maurice, Philip and Edward, who had been sent to Paris by Elizabeth to acquire some of the accomplishments they were unlikely to learn in the Hague, were put under a less restrictive arrest. While they grumbled about their situation and Charles

Louis fumed impotently in prison. Richelieu opened up negotiations with Erlach, the second in command to the late Duke of Saxe-Weimar, to buy the army. The army needed to be fed and was naturally willing to sell its services to the highest bidder. Richelieu came to terms and the conduct of the war therefore was no longer in the hands of the Germans but the French and, on the other side, the Hapsburgs. Germany merely became the battlefield.

By this time Richelieu was in a strong enough position to make a gesture of goodwill. He released Prince Maurice, who went scurrying back to his mother in the Hague, but he took much longer in letting the two younger brothers go. Charles Louis was by now so eager to be free—patience never having been his strong point—that he signed a declaration to the French King which even Elizabeth, despite herself, was rather ashamed of. "It is more than he should have done," she admitted, "but necessity has no law." When he had been released, Charles Louis tried to win Richelieu's support for his cause. In which he was sadly mistaken. The Cardinal's aim was to detach Bavaria from the Hapsburg alliance, with the bribe of Charles Louis' Palatine inheritance if need be. So *Son Eminence* feigned a certain interest and then made it clear that while England did nothing there was not much to be hoped for from him. Everything was blamed onto England. With this thought in mind Charles Louis returned to the Hague for a winter which proved to be "abominably cold".

The news that reached him from England must have given Charles Louis some reason to hope, although it would have given none to Rupert. Charles I was on the brink of bringing his country to civil war and his nephew, ensconced in furs and blankets in the Hague, decided to ingratiate himself with the Puritans in England in the hope of being given the throne if the situation got worse. The seeds of the trouble had been sown long ago when Buckingham had held so much influence over Charles I. Distrustful of Buckingham's policies and particularly the way he waged war with France and Spain, Parliament had kept their hands on the purse-strings. This, of course, was extremely awkward for the King and partly explained his inability to help his sister's family as much as he might otherwise have done. And then there had been the problem of religion. King Charles obviously disliked Puritanism and as he fell more and more deeply in love with his Roman Catholic Queen, there was growing concern that he might even go over to Rome. As his power weakened, he became more dogmatic on points of principle. If Parliament disagreed with him he would sooner dissolve it than alter his course. This he did in 1628 and then again in 1629. By then Buckingham was dead and Charles decided to rule by himself without Parliament for the next eleven years. Moreover he appointed William Laud, who belonged to the High Church, as Archbishop of Canterbury. Together they tried to unite the Church of England and Scotland in a way that showed a complete misunderstanding of the feelings of the Scots. So much so that there was a rebellion in Scotland. King Charles tried to quell it, failed, and, in order to raise enough money to support another campaign, was forced to recall Parliament. The second campaign was equally disastrous. The Scots were now calling for Elizabeth of Bohemia to be their queen.

King Charles had again dissolved Parliament and, before reopening it in 1640, had been forced to support his army by raising unfair taxes in whatever way he could think of. He thus sacrificed alliances which would have been useful to him in the future. Rumours soon began to proliferate that King Charles was about to raise troops in order to enforce his will on Parliament. His minister, the Earl of Strafford, was suspected of levying them. This led to Strafford's trial and eventually, with King Charles' sanction and to his eternal discredit, his execution. For a short time King Charles seemed to hold the balance in Parliament. In October 1641 the Irish, galvanised by the fear that, if the Puritans came to power, they would hand Irish land over to Scots and Englishmen, rose up in support of the King. King Charles saw it as an opportunity for testing his control over the army while the Opposition made it an excuse for passing through Parliament the Grand Remonstrance, which expressed Parliament's disapproval of all King Charles' policies since he had come to the throne in 1625.

The people of England were at heart sympathetic to the King

and they mistrusted the Opposition. However they had problems of their own to contend with during the winter of 1641. These were economic and they were blamed on the King. His methods of raising money over the last few years, the monopolies, the patents, the competition with the Dutch over fishing rights, trade in the Indies and freight, were all seen as his responsibility. Worse still during the past year they had seen him fraternising with the Dutch.

The fact was that for some time King Charles had seen trouble brewing and his thoughts had always been as much with his family as with his kingdom. The interests of these he felt would be served by marrying one of his daughters to the son of Frederick Henry of Orange. Holland was prosperous and could, if necessary, support King Charles with arms. Moreover, a daughter in a foreign Protestant court would afford some refuge for other members of his family if the need arose.

He did not tell his sister what he intended. He knew that she had always hoped, perhaps almost expected, that Charles Louis would marry his eldest daughter, Mary. In fact he had meant to marry her to the heir to the King of Spain. But these were troubled times and a princess was too significant a pawn in the field of diplomacy to be spent either on sentimentality or on the dream of sustaining peace with a country which was already on the decline. King Charles knew that Elizabeth would disapprove, but was not entirely aware of the reason. He suspected that she would feel such a marriage to someone who was not a crowned head would show how low he rated himself, but he did not appreciate that the influence of the Princess of Orange over Frederick Henry was already too pronounced and too much in favour of France and Spain not to undermine the independence of the Netherlands and therefore not to alienate the States General.

It was not until a fortnight before a statement was made to the States General that Elizabeth was told about the planned marriage. It was Amalia de Solms who came to tell her. The jubilant mother was full of apologies and excuses, which Elizabeth appeared to accept. But when she had left Elizabeth broke the news to Charles Louis making it quite clear that she was distressed by what she had been told. She then wrote to Sir Thomas Roe. "I cannot see what the King can gain, by precipitating this marriage. . . . They seek to get my eldest niece, but that I hope will not be granted, it is too low for her." She hoped the proposals concerned her namesake, Elizabeth, who was then only five years old and rather sickly. Charles Louis, in his turn, could not "conceive what should make the King precipitate the match." He was also annoyed about the conditions, particularly the suggestion that the bride should be brought up in the Orange Court. "Methinks next it is great sauciness in them to demand the breeding of so great a King's daughter," he countered. Morover he felt that his mother had been made a mockery of. "The concealing," he wrote, "of this business this long from the Queen, my mother, shows much distrust and little affection from the King, Queen or Prince of Orange to her, and consequently that little advantage will thereby befall her, since it seems she is in such a predicament with them, that they will not trust her with what concerns her nearest blood." Having said this Charles Louis with typical tactlessness set off for England. The Venetian Ambassador wrote about his arrival: "Although His Majesty in letters in his own hand, warned the Prince Palatine not to come to this court just now, he arrived here unexpectedly two days ago. He declares that he did not meet the courier sent and announces that the chief reason for his journey were the hopes of improving his own interests by his presence during the meeting of Parliament and the negotiation of the Dutch ambassadors. The King did not conceal his vexation at the news of his arrival, or the Queen either, but upon reflection they dissimulated their first feelings and received their nephew with the usual display of affection and esteem."

Charles Louis' reasons for coming were twofold. He hoped to secure some concessions for the Palatinate in the marriage treaty and he wanted to remind the Puritans in England of his existence.

By April, the fifteen-year-old Prince William had arrived in London. The treaty had stipulated that the wedding should take place in England and that Mary should go to Holland, not before she was twelve years old, to learn something of the Dutch people and their customs. She was to have English servants and she would practice her own religion. No mention was made of the Palatinate and King Charles even went so far as to suggest to the indignant young Elector Palatine that he might marry an Austrian, possibly the daughter of Leopold of Innsbruck. Charles Louis reacted by claiming precedence over the young bridegroom. This presumption was considered to be in very bad taste and for the remaining time that William was in England, Charles Louis was almost ignored.

King Charles' attention was divided instead between his troubles at home and Prince William, whom he liked well enough. The Orange Prince was potentially brilliant. He was fluent in several languages and an amasser of miscellaneous knowledge. However, as time went on, he would never quite succeed in anything he set out to do. Perhaps his melancholia was his chief handicap. Moreover he was haunted by a conviction that he was destined to die young. When he had been a child a horoscope prophesying that he would die in his twenty-fifth year and father a posthumous son had been presented to his mother. Amalia had been unable to trace the old woman who had pushed her way through the crowd to give it to her and she herself had taken little notice of its contents. However, unfortunately, she had relayed the prophecy to her son. From that day the horoscope was never far from his thoughts.

Mary resembled her mother. She was proud, even as a child, and the idea of the marriage was abhorrent to her. She looked down on Holland and never came to terms with the provincialism of the Dutch people. However she loved her family and had inherited some of the Stuart charm. Prince William was pleased with her and he wrote to his father: "At first we were sober in one another's company, but now we are very informal and relaxed; I find her much prettier than the paintings. I love her deeply, and I believe she loves me too." The marriage ceremony was very simple and soon after it Prince William returned to Holland to complete his education, while Mary remained with her family in England.

When Prince William came back to his home in the Binnenhof it was to find that Sophia, the youngest daughter of Elizabeth, was the constant and unpopular companion of his sisters. The grief she had suffered at the death of her nine-year-old brother Gustavus had made Sophia mischievous to the point of maliciousness. She believed to the end of her life that Gustavus would have lived but for the ineptitude of his doctors, who had failed to diagnose that he was suffering from a stone. With no companion at Leyden, she was brought to the Hague and once there she did her best to attract attention. To her, nothing was nearly as amusing as dipping her handkerchief in a chamberpot and flicking it into the face of one of her Orange cousins. When she was with her mother, she made endless efforts to win her admiration. But Elizabeth, grieving for her youngest son, became more interested in the fortunes of her elder ones: Charles Louis in England, Maurice fighting in the Upper Palatinate and Rupert. Sophia, precocious and craving for affection, she found rather tiresome.

Unlike his brother, Rupert had not come to anything that resembled dishonourable terms with his gaolers and consequently he was still in prison. The new Emperor had tried everything to discredit the obstinate young Palatine, but had failed. Hardly a day passed without some pressure being brought to bear. Would he become a Catholic? Would he apologise for his activities against the Emperor? Would he join the Emperor's forces? To all this Rupert remained adamant. He had already decided not to waste the time he was to spend in prison. Perhaps it would help him in later life if he did something worthwhile now. At least it would preserve his sanity. He began to sketch. He developed his interest in science by perfecting an instrument for getting the correct perspective in drawing. He trained a hare, and he flirted with the gaoler's daughter. In the end the Imperialists gave up hope of winning him over and he was set free on the flimsiest of unwritten promises that he would not fight against the Emperor's men. As there was likely to be war in England, it was not too tiresome a thing to have to agree to. Before returning home, Rupert was received in Vienna by the Emperor who entertained him with an exhausting round of banquets and excursions. It was with a feeling almost of reluctance that Rupert, visiting his birthplace at Prague on the way and the

—

149

Court of Saxony, at last set his course in the direction of Holland.

In the past Elizabeth had hardly given Rupert a fleeting thought, but now she had begun to pine for him. Perhaps she had spotted something of the intransigence and coldness in Charles Louis which had earned him the nickname of Timon the Cynic. She would not of course admit to such a thing. She hoped she was mistaken. Nevertheless she began to think of Rupert more than she had done and when her daughters were acting the *Tragedy of Medea and Jason* she suddenly saw in Louise, who played a man, a resemblance to Rupert which was so striking that she "would have justly called her by his name." It was nearly three years since he had been captured and when she heard that at last he was returning she admitted to Sir Thomas Roe: "I long to see Rupert here". By December she was writing anxiously, "I hear yet nothing of Rupert. He will have an ill journey, for it is extreme cold and a great snow here, and it must needs be worse where he shall pass." One evening soon afterwards Rupert burst in entirely unannounced while his mother was going through the ceremony which invariably preceded her sitting down to supper. He was, she decided, "not altered, only leaner, and grown". Only a few days passed before she was worrying about him again. What was his future to be? He could not, she conceded, go into battle against the Imperialists so soon after making his promise and, for some reason still uncertain about his honour, she was afraid to send him to England in case he might fall under the influence of Henrietta Maria. However, Rupert was determined to go to England as soon as the weather and courtesy enabled him to.

By December 1641 there had been rioting in London. The new Archbishop of York, John Williams, who had been appointed by the King, was hinted at having Catholic tendencies. Ireland was still in uproar and Pym was trying to force King Charles into some injudicious and premature action by circulating rumours that the Queen was about to be impeached. At this point King Charles tried to arrest the Five Members, while they were in Parliament. He was escorted by Charles Louis into the Chamber, but when they arrived the King had to admit! "All by birds have flown." It was a major humiliation. No longer did the King appear to be on the winning side. He began to make arrangements to send Henrietta Maria and Mary to Holland, ostensibly to fulfil the conditions of the marriage treaty.

In the meantime London was in revolt. Afraid for his life and above all the safety of his family, King Charles moved them to Hampton Court. Their arrival was so sudden that they all had to share the same bed.

Rupert arrived at Dover in February having tactfully put a rumour about that he was merely coming to thank the King for his efforts to obtain his release from prison and that, in the words of the Venetian Ambassador, "once he has performed this ceremonial duty he will return to his mother in Holland so as to avail giving any occasion for misgivings in his Majesty's mind by a longer stay here at a time of so much disturbance and innovation." He found King Charles preparing to say goodbye to Henrietta Maria and Mary. The King and Queen were both very different from when Rupert had last seen them. Van Dyck's elegant portraits, so full of grace and good looks, bore little resemblance to the middle-aged man, whose hair was streaked with grey and whose anxieties were revealed by the lines of tension around his mouth, and the small, frightened Queen, whom Rupert's youngest sister would soon describe as "a thin little woman with shrunken arms, and teeth sticking out of her mouth like guns from a fort." Rupert told his uncle that he was willing to do anything to help. To his intense disappointment he found himself escorting Henrietta Maria and Mary to Holland with instructions to raise arms and money there. One Palatine in England was enough, King Charles felt, although he would have been glad to have Rupert in Charles Louis' stead.

The Elector Palatine had been nothing but a trial since his arrival. Moreover he seemed cursed with bad luck. He had broken his arm riding, he was so impoverished that he was pawning his possessions to buy the correct clothes, he sulked and, worst of all, King Charles guessed correctly that he was waiting to see which way the wind would blow before committing himself either to his uncle or to Parliament.

There were no such doubts about Rupert, who set sail with

Henrietta Maria and Mary on 23 February 1642. The King and Queen parted in tears and, until the details of the coast were no longer visible, the passengers saw the King riding along the cliffs looking out to sea to catch a last glimpse of his wife.

The journey across the Channel seemed almost bereft of hope. Among the Queen's luggage, Rupert knew, were the Crown Jewels and the personal jewelry of his uncle and aunt. It was not something he would tell his mother.

The Holland the ship was approaching was probably the most materially secure country in the world. It was a nation now of immaculate houses, frugality and confidence. Above all it was a nation of burghers—governed to all purposes by the regent-burghers who were chosen to represent the eighteen large towns in Holland in the States General. The Stathouder acted as an overseer and his power, which could be extensive, relied on his personality and popular esteem.

But, in spite of the prosperity, there was an underlying political discontent. Frederick Henry was rapidly losing his popularity as well as the strength to regain it. It was rumoured that his wife had leanings towards France and Spain and this was abhorred. As her husband grew older and wrestled alternatively with bouts of jaundice and gout, it was Amalia who did his work. Lying in bed reading books on military science, Frederick Henry neglected his subjects' petitions. Only the marriage between his son, Prince William, and the King of England's eldest daughter diverted his attention from his books, for the truth was that by middle age Frederick Henry had become a snob. He saw himself as a dynast and sometimes when his sense of humour deserted him he rather regretted that he himself had not married better. He did his best to make his daughter-in-law and her mother welcome in Holland. The ship coming from England was joined by the Dutch fleet, headed by Admiral van Tromp, who escorted it to Brill. There the English Queen and Princess were met by the Prince of Orange and his son and Elizabeth and her daughters, La Grecque, Henrietta and Sophia, who were enjoying a rare outing.

Stepping out of her coach, which was lined with crimson velvet, Elizabeth regarded her sister-in-law appraisingly and was quick to notice four Roman Catholic priests among her entourage. She greeted Henrietta Maria with a certain degree of reservation. "The Queen doth govern all the King's affairs," she had written only recently and rather bitterly to Sir Thomas Roe. It was true, but Elizabeth soon overcame her feelings of disquiet and the two queens were very civil to one another. Henrietta Maria had soon won over Sophia, too, by comparing her with Mary. "Still, after careful inspection," Sophia conceded, "I found she had beautiful eyes, a well-shaped nose, and an admirable complexion." But wasn't there, Elizabeth felt, something uncompromising underneath the charming brittle veneer? Wasn't there also something pathetic and ill-judged?

As if her situation was not bad enough, Henrietta Maria had soon realised that the power of the Stathouder, for which she had sacrificed her daughter, was by no means as comprehensive as she had believed. The burghers decided on Dutch foreign policy and they, to her horror, favoured Parliament. At the first banquet the English Queen attended, a murmur of disapproval had reverberated through the hall when the toasts were proposed: to Henrietta Maria first, then to Frederick Henry and finally to the States General. "He's a servant in our pay," one of the burghers had whispered too audibly to be ignored. "We are his masters," others chimed in. There had been an embarrassed pause until a French Captain of the Horse retorted: "A prince who has just married his son to a daughter of England, grand-daughter of France, should be ashamed to pass for a servant of brewers, bakers and feltmakers." The response to this, as far as Henrietta Maria could discern, was something along the lines that, if that was the case, Frederick Henry should look elsewhere for a princedom.

As the days went by it was becoming increasingly difficult for Henrietta Maria to muster even a wry flicker of a smile or a wave for the crowds who peered inquisitively through the windows of her carriage and soon all the charm she could evoke was being expended on people who might give her money or arms for her husband and particularly on ambassadors of countries which might become his allies. From every quarter she struggled to get assistance. From the King of Denmark, from Frederick Henry, from France; but it was almost impossible for her to sustain a façade of geniality, and the impression she gave all too often was one of desperation.

Everything seemed to go against her. Parliament issued a notice concerning the Crown Jewels which made it difficult to pawn them and Henrietta Maria found herself very much at the mercy of the brokers as far as her personal jewels were concerned. "You may judge how," she wrote to King Charles, "when they know we want money, they keep their foot on our throat." Moreover, throughout her stay in Holland her ordeal was aggravated by dreadful toothache. "I hardly know what I am doing," she wrote, the pain was so bad. Everything about Holland she found depressing. "I need the air of England," she complained and Elizabeth, looking across the provincial waterways which flanked the Vijerberg and the Binnenhof, understood that, too.

The Winter Queen spent long patient hours with this dolorous companion, and the more time she spent the more anxious she became about Rupert.

In April King Charles sent the Garter insignia to him to express his gratitude and to secure Rupert's support. Elizabeth cautiously suggested to her son that it might be a good idea if he served Venice instead. But he was already too deeply embroiled and nothing would divert him. Nevertheless, these months in the Hague were a time of discontent for him. How he envied Charles Louis in England, although the reports that reached him of his brother's activities, losing money at cards to his uncle and hunting, were scarcely more exciting than his own in Holland and certainly less constructive. When the action did come, Charles Louis promptly deserted his uncle in favour of the Parliamentarians, leaving the Palatine brothers as divided among themselves as England itself.

As the situation deteriorated, Henrietta Maria persisted with her efforts. The Stathouder, despite the open support the Dutch Estates were giving to Parliament, was generously, but not too obviously, providing money from his private funds to buy arms for

King Charles. By July a large sum of money, as well as pistols, carbines, six cannons, barrels of powder and some firelocks, had been amassed. It was these arms that gave Rupert the excuse he needed for going to England. Even this was not easy. The coast was so well patrolled by the navy, which was on the side of the Roundheads, that he was forced back to the Netherlands and at the second attempt he only very narrowly eluded them and raced into Tynemouth. The journey had made him thoroughly ill, but he insisted on wasting no time before joining the King. Everything in him craved for action. With Maurice he set off for Nottingham, but he was in such a hurry that he fell from his horse and dislocated his shoulder. By the time he reached his destination King Charles was in Coventry. At Coventry Rupert missed him again. Eventually they met at Leicester and then at last he could embark on his career as one of the most dashing soldiers in history. He was given the post of General of the Horse. Not surprisingly there were problems to begin with. German by upbringing and Czech by birth, he did not appreciate the subtleties of fighting in a civil war in an England unused to military activity. He promptly demanded £2,000 from the citizens of Leicester in return for not sacking the city. This came at a time when the majority of Englishmen were still undecided as to which side they would take, and naturally the Parliamentarians made the most of the story. It was one of very few mistakes and, despite Henrietta Maria's assertion that Rupert was "self-willed", he was soon the hero of the Cavaliers.

This was not without cost to his family in the Hague. The support given to King Charles by Rupert and Maurice meant that Elizabeth could no longer depend on England for money. Charles Louis, particularly, was anxious to absolve himself from the suspicion of any collusion with Rupert. His behaviour had nothing to do with him, he stressed time and again. "It is impossible," he announced, "either for the Queen my mother or myself to bridle my brother's youth and fieryness, at so great a distance and in the employment he has."

Elizabeth was compelled to face the impossible dilemma. Of course she favoured her brother and of course she hated Parliament.

But there was so little she could do to help him and that at such great cost to herself. None of her daughters had married and they had to be provided for. There had been offers: the Elector of Brandenburg had expressed an interest in Louise and King Charles had encourgaged him asserting that the Palatine House would soon be restored, "its former greatness being now more earnestly taken in hand and more confidently hoped than heretofore." But William of Brandenburg, more prudently than he would have liked, had now turned his attention to another Louise, the eldest rather melancholy daughter of the Stathouder. Louise had had other suitors including Prince Radziwell, and many admirers, but nothing ever seemed to come to anything where the Palatine princesses were concerned. A suggestion that Sophia, being the same age as the Prince of Wales, might marry him, had hardly been taken seriously by anyone except Amalia de Solms and Sophia herself. As for the eldest, La Grecque, she had become so immersed in her studies and the company of the middle-aged philosopher Descartes that it seemed improbable that she would ever attract a husband now.

Charles Louis, despairing of his sisters, was doing his best to marry off his brothers for financial gain. He still hoped for a marriage between one of them and the rich Mademoiselle de Rohan. "I know that my brother Rupert," he was writing desperately in 1643, "hath an aversion to that match, whereof I know not the cause; if that continue, I pray let me know whether my brother Maurice will put for it or in case he also neglect it, my brother Edward will endeavour it, for such a likely advantage to our family is not to be lost." But Maurice felt the same as Rupert and Edward had other plans.

Elizabeth was therefore left with her entire family dependent on her and the threat of all her money from England being cut off. Even running her household was expensive and the master of it, Sir Charles Cottrell, had long ago implemented as many economies as he could think of. "Touching the English Beer," he had admonished the kitchen staff, "He [the Cellarer] shall spare it as much as possibly he can, and give none to any other than for the Princes, the Princesses, ladies and gentlemen. . . . The common sort, and the workmen" would have to be content with the ordinary Hague beer. "The Baker," he continued, "shall give nobody meats for the pies, tarts, buns or sauces, unless he bring a bill from the Clerk of the Kitchen. . . . The waiting men shall lock up diligently the cheese after every meal and keep away from the cats and rats."

Recently people had noticed a marked increase in the rat population of the Wassaenor Hof, scuttling behind the faded hangings and even, it was said, hidden under the skirts of the sad old Winter Queen when a visitor came to see her. But Elizabeth seldom entertained at all now. Most of her time was spent at her writing desk, thinking of ways in which she might alleviate her worsening financial position. She realised that she must compromise and ill-informed observers even believed that she supported the Parliamentarians. But sometimes her real loyalties would reveal themselves and she would write encouragingly to her brother or to Rupert. Then repercussions would invariably follow. "Sir," she was having to write to the Speaker of the House of Commons in April 1643, "Having understood, by imperfect reports, of the interception of some letters which I wrote occasionally to the king, and my son, whereat the Parliament had taken offence, I cannot be at rest till I have endeavoured to remove all such impressions as might deprive me of their good opinion." But the good opinion of the Puritans had been forfeited the moment Rupert had landed on English soil vowing to give all he had to the King of England. "The Pearl of Britain", as they had once called her, was now no more than the King's sister, far from glamorous and even at times having recourse to the use of spectacles, begging for money which could be more profitably spent on armaments.

Elizabeth considered ways in which she might appease Parliament. She dismissed her chaplain, Dr Samson Johnson, a difficult man whose religious beliefs were more extreme than Archbishop Laud's and who had long been a source of controversy in the Hague. Up to now Elizabeth had defended him. He had not been entirely loyal in return, referring on paper to Elizabeth as "of a gracious and facile nature, often to her prejudice", and verbally in rather less cordial terms.

Charles Louis went further. He went to Parliament and offered to serve them in any way he could. Elizabeth certainly found this galling and it was only with a loss of pride that she accepted the small sums of money the Parliament did send her. They were not even enough to cover her household expenses and she began to rely heavily for money on the adoring and rich William, Lord Craven, and to apply to the Dutch States for long-term loans.

All this was not lost on Henrietta Maria. Her sister-in-law's continual quest for allies and money reminded her not unnaturally of her own cajoling with ambassadors from France and Denmark and her wrangling with the jewellers in Amsterdam. Moreover the news from England hurt them both equally. "You may well imagine," Elizabeth was writing to Sir Thomas Roe in January 1643, "how much the miseries of our country trouble me, and I can hope for no good change yet. The Queen is preparing to go for England with the first wind; she continues still her kindness and civilities to me."

Henrietta Maria left her daughter Mary in the Hague. The child had already grown fond of her aunt, who referred to her as "my best niece". She had also already taken a strong dislike to her mother-in-law, Amalia. It was not unjustified. Amalia was obviously jealous of her daughter-in-law who, she felt, had usurped her. Whenever Mary was present, Frederick Henry would deferentially take his hat off and in such gestures Amalia was reminded that she herself was not of royal blood. After her mother left Holland, Mary was put in charge of her own household. She was only eleven and, because her father-in-law and her husband were both often away fighting the Spanish, she felt lonely and isolated. She spent a great deal of time with Elizabeth, asking her advice and confiding in her. Elizabeth enjoyed her company and felt more of an affinity with the eldest daughter of the King of England beset with the problems of a hostile mother-in-law than with her own daughters. It was a fatal combination. Elizabeth could never disguise her contempt for the Dutch people and their puritanical habits, retiring promptly as they did at 10 o'clock, and their subjugation of pleasure for a life of domesticity. And so unwittingly she fostered in her daughter-in-law a dislike of her future subjects and an inflated sense of self-importance.

November was taken up with the festivities celebrating Mary's twelfth birthday. For once Elizabeth was not with her. The news that Maurice was suffering from a stone and in danger of his life had made her ill.

CHAPTER THIRTEEN

Maurice recovered, but reports from England brought no better news than that. Battles and strongholds lost to the Roundheads had brought King Charles to the brink of defeat. For Elizabeth the defeats meant that her money from England was cut off. Life at the Hague, now alive with political activity, became almost unbearable. In January she had pleurisy, in March a very bad cold, in June she was confined to her room for three weeks because of ill-health. The young Elizabeth and Sophia were also ill and there were even doubts at one stage that the latter would recover. Nothing would have cured them so quickly as good news, but none came.

In March Louisa Juliana died leaving Elizabeth a message of reconciliation. "Write to the Queen of Bohemia," had been almost her last request to her daughter, "and bid her adieu from me. I shall never see her in this world; but I pray God that she may yet see many years of happiness and receive His blessing. Tell her that I had always loved and honoured her." Throughout the years of exile Louisa Juliana had been writing letters of encouragement to Elizabeth. She had refrained from blaming her in any way for what had happened and they had sustained a cordial relationship by letter. They had not seen each other since Frederick and Elizabeth had left for Bohemia, but nevertheless Elizabeth had developed a feeling of affection for the pious old lady, who, despite all her misfortunes, had never ceased to believe that everything would be happily resolved by God. Elizabeth arranged for Louisa Juliana's chaplain, the German historian Spanheim, to compile a life of her mother-in-law and in time she even began to miss those letters so full of confidence in the divine will.

She had always relied on correspondence. Letters had been her only means of escaping from her grim confinement at the Hague. She had poured much more of her thoughts out onto paper, particularly to Henry's old friend Sir Thomas Roe, than may have been wise. But now even Roe was dying. His letters had been full of bad news about his health for some years. In 1639 Elizabeth had sent him a stone which she had acquired from Dr Rumpf "for your infirmities" and since then she had been urging him to take care of himself, and to consult a good physician. He had hardly heeded her advice, scouring Europe at his usual speed in a hopeless quest for allies and useful contacts.

The deaths of these two avid letter writers were not compensated by letters from children abroad. She had grown almost wary of opening letters from Charles Louis, full as they were of advice and rebuke. Rupert seldom wrote, but when he did the pages were characteristically covered in splodges, which exasperated his mother. Maurice wrote even less often and the two youngest boys, Edward and Philip, who, to their mother's indignation had not even bothered to make a courtesy call to the Doge when they were in Venice, wrote so dully that she did not mind that she heard from them infrequently. Edward and Philip were, she decided, rather a disappointment. The events of 1645 and 1646 strengthened this belief.

Edward was the best looking of her sons. Moreover his manners, which he had cultivated in the court of the Queen-Regent in France, were actually a source of pride to his mother. There was none of Rupert's soldierly nonchalance about his appearance: almost too much the reverse. While he was in Paris he had fallen in love with Anne of Gonzaga, the second daughter of Duke Charles of Gonzaga-Nevers. She was eight years older than Edward and much more sophisticated. He was twenty-one. A contemporary wrote that Anne was "Mistress of her own will, she saw the world, and was seen by it; soon she felt how much she pleased, and there is no need to tell the subtle poison that vanity instilled into her young heart."

When she first met Edward she had been in love with Henry of Guise, but he rejected her and, on the rebound, she agreed to marry Edward on condition that he changed his religion and became a Catholic. To him it seemed a small price to pay, but his mother, when she heard that both the marriage and the conversion had taken place, was horrified. Henrietta Maria, who was now in Paris, was believed to have encouraged the match and this caused a rift between her and Elizabeth, who announced that she would have preferred to have been dead than to have seen one of her children become a Catholic. The young Elizabeth took the same view as her mother and Charles Louis wrote rather awkwardly from England, where he was again making up to Parliament, that he didn't believe Edward's conversion could be genuine. This view was not justified by events. Edward never deviated from his new religion. Moreover his marriage turned out happily and, unlike his brothers and sisters, he lived a prosperous and contented life. His wife's money meant that he never again had to apply to his mother for financial help, and Elizabeth, in her turn, grateful to be alleviated of one financial burden, in due course received him in the Hague. For the time being she hoped they would never cross paths again. She began now to worry about her other children, particularly Philip, who had also been partly educated in France. Might he also be thinking of adopting the abhorred religion? Charles Louis, who had prompted her fears, found employment for him elsewhere, but not for long enough. The following year he acted in a way that made Edward's conduct seem inconsequential.

Elizabeth was now a rather stout middle-aged lady. Ill-health and anxiety had destroyed the last vestiges of her beauty. Louise, when she painted her mother, made her look almost ugly, in a neckline still lower than her daughters wore and clothes more suited to the Jacobean era than to the 1640s. It was therefore not really surprising that when a handsome young Frenchman, Lieutenant-colonel Jaques de l'Epinay, Sieur de Vaux, arrived in the Hague full of what must have seemed like a refreshing amount of sophistication, wit and flattery, Elizabeth rather took to him. It was no more than that. She was bored and he amused her. Her daughter, Louise, also found him amusing and he carried on a flirtation with both the mother and daughter. What Elizabeth chose to ignore was the fact that de l'Epinay had come to "the largest village in Europe" as the Hague was rather aptly called, not from choice, but from necessity. In Paris he was notorious for his amorous exploits and some incident which had thoroughly reinforced his reputation had driven him to the Hague. Charles Louis and the young Elizabeth both thought him insolent and, on one occasion, the former had knocked off the young French officer's hat while he was walking with it on in the company of Elizabeth. The fact that it was raining was not considered an excuse for this signal of disrespect. When Charles Louis left the Hague for England, Philip took up the cause. He saw de l'Epinay for what he was, and he had probably heard about his antics in Paris. He requested him to stop seeing his sister and his mother. De l'Epinay ridiculed him and spoke meaningfully of his *bonnes fortunes* with Elizabeth and Louise. Philip challenged him to a duel, which, in the event was interrupted before it could take place. The following day Philip, still incensed, saw him in the market place and killed him with a hunting-knife. Whether or not de l'Epinay himself was armed or had any chance in the fight is not recorded. No trial ever took place, because as soon as the crime had been committed, the youngest Palatine prince drove post-haste to the frontier and only returned when the threat of proceedings had been dropped.

Several Frenchmen vowed to avenge their countryman and Elizabeth herself reportedly expressed the hope that she would never see her son again. The murder had done more harm to her reputation than all her walks in the park. People began to wonder if there might have been something in the rumours after all.

On this issue, as on so many others, the family took different sides. La Grecque staunchly supported her brother. Charles Louis, who only a few weeks before had written to his mother "I hope before my brother Philip parts, that your Majesty will, with your blessings, lay your curse upon him if he change the religion he hath been bred in", now begged her not to condemn her son and in so doing divide the family. Elizabeth, after the initial shock, did not openly speak badly of her youngest son. Instead she hardly mentioned him at all. He had in his own way humiliated her. Of course he had meant to do quite the reverse, but the result was something Elizabeth would find hard to forgive.

The news of Rupert was also distressing. Affairs in England had gone from bad to worse. Rupert's defeat by the troops of Oliver Cromwell at Marston Moor had shattered his reputation. The subsequent disastrous defeat at Naseby, although it was not his doing since King Charles had by then taken to acting on the advice of more optimistic and less realistic counsellors, left Rupert with little opportunity of any of the inspiring victories which had marked his early career. In September 1645 Rupert had been compelled to surrender Bristol. He had actually put up the white flag fractionally earlier than may have been necessary in order to save the lives of the garrison. In the eyes of the King this was tantamount to treason.

"Though the loss of Bristol be a great blow to me," King Charles had written to his nephew, "yet your surrendering it as you did is of so much affliction to me that it makes me not only forget the consideration of that place, but is likewise the greatest trial of my constancy that hath yet befallen me. For what is to be done after one that is so near me as you are, both in blood and friendship, submits himself to so mean an action? . . . my conclusion is to desire you to seek your subsistence, until it shall please God to determine of my condition, somewhere beyond seas." A court martial later found him innocent and King Charles had to retract his words. However, Rupert was never restored to his command, perhaps because the war was so obviously lost that no command was left.

Rupert waited in England for the inevitable end, which came when in May 1646 King Charles surrendered to the Scots at Newark and was sealed when in June Oxford was surrendered. He and Maurice then left England and while Maurice made his way to the Hague where he intended to regain his health completely, Rupert went to France to fight there.

Maurice found the Wassaenor Hof as sombre as ever. The young Elizabeth was just setting off for Berlin, largely it was suspected because her absence would relieve the financial burden on her mother. The eldest daughter of the Prince of Orange had recently married the Elector of Brandenburg and visiting her gave La Grecque a slender, but respectable, excuse for going to Germany.

That winter in the Hague was the coldest for thirty years. The shortage of money was as obvious as ever. Maurice soon learnt that, not only was his mother petitioning to Parliament, but her creditors were as well. Any money that was available for the Palatines in fact came from property which had been confiscated either from King Charles himself or from some of his loyal followers. Most of this went to Charles Louis. He was living comfortably enough in England where he spread largesse among various artists and poets. Like his mother, who admired the paintings of Rubens and Honthorst and had studied the new tonal technique of chiascuro, and like his uncle, he had a genuine love of paintings. However, Elizabeth felt certain misgivings about the way Charles Louis spent the money which had been misappropriated from her brother, particularly as he sent none to her. As time went by rumours began to spread about Charles Louis' love affairs. According to those reports, his life seemed to be in marked contrast to the dreariness of the Hague.

The Golden Age of Holland was already on the decline. An air of despondency pervaded the Hague. Everyone knew that Frederick Henry was dying. He had been the best loved of William the Silent's sons and he had instilled a feeling of security into the States. He was, according to one contemporary, "so mild that he would not willingly hurt a sparrow" and yet strong enough to command his armies with rare skill. He was the first Stathouder not to speak Dutch with a foreign accent and somehow he had steered a straight course through the varying factions that wrangled for power in Holland. For some time he had been incapable of making decisions and finally, racked with the agonising illness which had made his last years so ineffectual, he died in March 1647. In him Elizabeth lost a loyal friend.

Without Frederick Henry's wisdom and moderation it was difficult for the somewhat anomalous position of the Stathouder to be maintained. Very little real power was vested in the position and it was only because of the 1631 Act of Reversion, which had been passed in deference to Frederick Henry, that William II was granted the Stathouderate at all. The States General took a year to confirm him in it. They saw that William was quite unlike his father. He was extravagant and pretentious and this was encouraged by his wife who told him, in words reminiscent of Elizabeth herself, that she considered it a degradation not to be a queen.

By the summer of 1647 La Grecque had returned to the Hague. She had found Brandenburg not only sandy and water-logged, but also devastated by the war. She had missed her discussions with Descartes about philosophy and she was sorry to find when she returned that he was in Stockholm. "I am moreover convinced," he had written to her while she was in Germany, "that if you had not been where you now are, I should never have been known in those regions." In return he did his best to interest Christina of Sweden in the Palatines' cause, but he had always been rather gauche in his human relationships—avoiding as he did social contact as much as possible—and never more so than now. The young Christina was herself famed for her learning. She was known throughout Europe as Pallas Nordica, a title which had been earned by her knowledge of at least eight languages and her rather shallow, but nevertheless precocious, interest in a variety of other subjects. She valued her reputation and she wanted it to remain unrivalled. The eldest Palatine daughter was obviously a serious threat and when, on the suggestion of Descartes, she wrote a letter hinting that she might come to Sweden, the Swedish Queen snubbed her in the most effective way she could think of. She totally ignored the letter. Elizabeth, who had been shopping in the Hague for suitable clothes to take with her to Stockholm, waited anxiously for the reply which never came. In the end she decided that the letter must have been mislaid. That seemed the only plausible explanation. For so long she had heard Gustavus Adolphus's daughter praised that now she could believe no wrong of her. But her mother was less credulous. She saw Christina's behaviour as a rebuff for the whole Palatine family and, although she always relished the gossip that surrounded the young Swedish Queen, she never forgave her.

Besides the situation in Europe very soon reached the point where Elizabeth could dispense with the Swedes. Charles Louis under the Treaty of Westphalia had been restored to the Lower Palatinate. The Upper Palatinate remained with Bavaria, but there was a stipulation that, if Maximilian's line were to die out, that territory should be reabsorbed into Charles Louis' lands. For this Charles Louis was compelled to renounce all other claim to the rest of the Palatinate and to accept, not the first Electorship of the Empire, but the Eighth. Elizabeth was far from pleased with the terms. At best they were a compromise and at worst a defeat, but Charles Louis made the best of them. He issued a medal with himself beside the Palatine lion and the words *Cedendo non cedo* inscribed. Throughout Germany there was as much general rejoicing as was possible in a country so depleted.

> *We have deserved nothing*, wrote Paul Gerhardt resignedly,
> *But heavy penalty and great wrath,*
> *Because there still flourishes*
> *Among us the fresh and mean tree of sin.*

But in fact nothing, not even sin, could flourish amid such lassitude and devastation. The population had in some places been halved. In their quest for food the survivors had resorted to dragging corpses from graves to eat. Homes had been pillaged and burnt, commerce had been annihilated. Moreover, after so much sacrifice, nothing had been achieved. There had merely been a weakening of powers in Germany.

As far as religion was concerned, the Treaty used as its criterion the position as it had been on 1 January 1624. Whatever the situation had been in each region on that date, with some slight variations, it was to revert to after the signing of the Treaty. This of course included Bohemia, which had very early on been forced to submit to Roman Catholicism. The toll on her population was as terrible as anywhere else. Frederick had had 3,000,000 subjects in Bohemia when he was crowned, now the country, deprived of its independence, had a mere 800,000 inhabitants.

Moreover the dynasty which had quelled the vigour of the Bohemians had also forfeited its own place on the European stage. The Hapsburgs in Madrid and in Vienna were no longer as strong as the Bourbons in France. Hardly had the ink dried in the treaty than commentators saw a new and no less ominous pattern forming in Europe. For the time being however they turned their attention to England.

The events in Germany over the last thirty years made those in England appear almost insignificant. Nevertheless there was growing concern about the fate of King Charles. By the autumn of 1648 he had accepted, even if his friends had not, that his death was virtually inevitable. He expected to be quietly assassinated and what he sought to do before that happened was to save the power of the monarchy. He was a prisoner on the Isle of Wight, living in the style of a learned country gentleman of moderate means. Surreptiously, however, he was continually plotting. The dreariness of his imprisonment was punctuated by reports of abortive risings in his cause and the deaths of his supporters. Parliament had no intention of stopping the bloodshed. "A list of divers Persons whose Names are to be presented to the King's majesty, to Die without Mercy", included the names of Rupert, Maurice and the Earl of Montrose. Each list conjured up well-loved faces and memories to the middle-aged King, but he held to his purpose. Nothing mattered to him now except his eldest son's accession to absolute power and he was grateful for the knowledge that Prince Charles, having failed to rout his father's enemies, was now safe in the Hague with his brother James, who had escaped from England dressed as a woman. There they were encouraged in a series of fruitless schemes by Elizabeth and her children.

Henrietta Maria was equally well-meaning but ineffectual. She was still in Paris and she had not seen her husband since 1644. Now his letters were so closely censored that she could not communicate straightforwardly with him. Her only consolation was that he still relied on her. "I must be a close prisoner," King Charles wrote to the Marquis of Ormonde on 28 October 1648, "Wherefore I must command you two things; first to obey all my wife's commands; then not to obey any command of mine until I send you word that I am free from restraint."

That time, as he suspected, would never come. The ensuing trial of the King was merely a formality. Elizabeth, in the Hague, hearing with horror the news she read in broadsheets smuggled out of England of the trial and its progress, prepared to go to see her brother. But even if she had been able to set out at once, Parliament would have prevented her. As it was she never had time even to plan the journey. King Charles had been condemned to death. His friends and family abroad did everything they could to save him. Prince Charles sent three pieces of blank paper with his signature at the bottom so that Parliament could fill in any terms they wanted. Henrietta Maria begged Parliament to allow her to visit him, but they did not even open her letter. The States General of Holland pleaded for his life and Louis XIV signed a document which referred to the Roundheads in Parliament as "A small handful of the basest of people", and went on to "declare our detestation of all such proceedings; and vow, in the presence of God and his holy angels a full revenge upon all actors or abettors of this odious design." The words were strong, but the threats were empty. Parliament knew this and proceeded. They fixed the date for the King's execution for 30 January. On 29 January Charles saw the two of his children, Elizabeth and Henry, who were still in England, but refused a visit from Charles Louis, who was waiting outside the prison. In his will he left nothing to his sister or to any of her children. It was so many years since he had seen her that she was really little more than a stranger to him. He saw briefly her picture among those of his family as he walked through Whitehall on 30 January, but by now he was thinking only of his death and his martyrdom. "I go from a corruptible to an incorruptible Crown, where no disturbance can be, no disturbance in the world," he said just before he was executed.

The block, he noticed, was very low. He was uncertain why this should be, but probably guessed that Parliament, afraid that he might resist, were even at this late stage taking precautions. They fatally misjudged him. Whatever his faults, since he had been a child, he had consistently displayed outstanding physical courage. He was also something of an actor and unlikely to forsake his dignity at such a critical moment. Standing amid his subjects for the last time he may have recalled the words his father had written while still in Scotland: "A King is as one set on a scaffold, whose smallest actions and gestures all the people do gazingly behold . . . the people who seeth but the outward part, will ever judge of the substance by the circumstances." He could not have gone to his death more calmly or indeed more confident of the justice of his cause. No sooner had the axe fallen than it was clear that the cult of Charles the Martyr, so skilfully nurtured by the King himself, was taking hold. People fought to dip their handkerchiefes in his blood and to find relics. It made Parliament wary. They refused to have him buried in Henry VII's Chapel with his parents in case this might attract demonstrators. Instead he was interred at Windsor in a vault where Henry VIII and Jane Seymour, having done their best to continue the Tudor line, had long ago been laid to rest.

CHAPTER FOURTEEN

Rupert was at sea when his uncle died. With a small squadron he had relieved the Royalists blockaded in Jersey on his way with supplies for the Royalists in Ireland. He vowed to "take vengeance upon those Arch-traitors, pretending the name of Parliament."

Other people denounced Parliament's action with equal fervour. "An act so transcendantly abominable," was how Sir Edward Nicholas recorded it.

Elizabeth for her part saw Cromwell as "the beast in the Revelations". And yet she partly blamed herself. She had never imagined that Parliament could have come to this. Might it have been different, she asked herself time and again, if she had supported her brother more completely? Might perhaps her voice have just altered the balance? She would never know, but whatever the answer she never again pandered to Parliament. As a constant reminder of her brother, she carried with her a lock of his greying hair encased in a mourning ring. Every year she observed the anniversary of his death. It was not always easy. On one occasion one of Cromwell's spies reported gloatingly that when Elizabeth and other residents at the Hague went to the Church on the anniversary of the execution they were ordered to leave. When they refused to do so a messenger from the States General told them that he had been ordered to lock them in if they did not comply. Rather ignominiously they were forced to go to Princess Mary's rooms.

For some time news from England almost completely dominated the courts of Europe. Every week Elizabeth scoured the pamphlets

which were smuggled across the Channel to the Hague. The story
was always the same, only the reporting varied.

> *O! Murther Murther is the thing*, one dispatch read,
> *That traitors do devise*
> *They first did kill their Lord and King*
> *And subjects now likewise* . . . .

The King's murder had not marked the end of the carnage.
Few royalists in England were safe. A clergyman who prayed for
King Charles II was condemned as a traitor and throughout 1649
the bloodshed continued. Abroad there was general hostility
towards the Parliamentarians. King Charles II's contemporary,
Tsar Alexis of Russia, threw the English merchants into prison and
confiscated their goods. In France many English imports were
banned. Throughout Europe Roundheads were murdered in
foreign courts. The most notable of these was Isaac Dorislaus who
came as an ambassador from Cromwell to the States General.
He had been Parliamentary counsel at King Charles' trial and The
Hague he was sent to was seething with Royalist refugees. Within a
week of his arrival he had been murdered by a follower of the
Marquis of Montrose.

Montrose himself was a focal point for Royalist intrigue. He had
been converted to the King's cause in 1640 and since then had been
inciting the Highlanders in Scotland against the Scottish army
which was fighting for Parliament. He was brave, and determined,
in his own words, for King Charles to:

> . . . *sing thine obsequies in trumpet sounds,*
> *And write thine epitaph in blood and wounds.*

Elizabeth found some comfort in the presence of Montrose at the
Hague. Their views concurred and she could confide in him. They
both shared the fear that the young King Charles might come to
some agreement with the Covenanters in Scotland and, in so
diminishing the power of the Crown, effectively betray his father's
cause. Hour after hour Elizabeth was able to discuss the political
situation with this chivalrous Scots soldier and, when he left the

Hague, she continued these debates by letter. She saw him once again when he came to Rhenen in late August 1649 to "walk and shoot". The correspondence did not continue long after that.

The success of Cromwell's troops in Ireland, if anything so brutal can ever be considered entirely successful, had driven the young and inexperienced King into a compromise with the Covenanters in Scotland which involved his renouncing Montrose. It was just this sort of situation that Elizabeth and Montrose had dreaded and it cost Montrose his life. He had returned to Scotland to raise the Highlands in the Royalists' cause. He had been captured and vilely executed in Edinburgh.

Elizabeth kept his portrait, which had been painted by Honthorst. It hung amid the fading tapestries and draughty corridors of the Wassaenor Hof. She felt that it deserved a better setting, but there was little hope of any reupholstering in the near future. Even her stables were being disbanded now. By early March 1649 she was petitioning to the States General for money, suspecting that she could not rely on Charles Louis to support her once he was established in Heidelberg.

Her financial position was particularly embarrassing because she was having to rely so much on Lord Craven for money. Craven, who had fought with Charles Louis on his first campaign, was regarded as a figure of fun by the younger Palatines. Deeply in love with Elizabeth, who was considerably older than he was, he longed to excel in wit and wisdom and to win her admiration. Elizabeth in return was grateful to him for his generosity, but that was all.

Unfortunately Craven was soon trapped by an agent provocateur into declaring his Royalist sympathies and his estates in England had been forfeited. His income was therefore severely curtailed. This plunged Elizabeth into even deeper financial difficulties at a time when the Court of Orange was filled with Royalists whom she would have liked to assist. Until shortly after the murder of Dorislaus, Charles and the Duke of York were there with their various followers; but it was a young court which had little room for the ageing Winter Queen, who found herself more often a spectator than a participant to the goings-on.

William and Mary were deeply in love and their life seemed to involve an endless pursuit of amusing diversions. William for his part was not entirely faithful to his wife. "I know she loves me as her own soul and I care for her more than anyone in the world," he would say, "but one can't live in such constraint all the time." By 1650 Mary was expecting a child. The quarrels which reverberated through the Binnenhof became more persistent. Moreover there were political issues which added to the tension. William, unlike the States General, had wanted after the Treaty of Westphalia to continue the war against Spain in order to regain parts of the Spanish Netherlands. As well as this, he had intended to help Charles I in England. To assert his authority he made an issue of the fact that Amsterdam had a standing army. He led some men against the town with the result that, although on the face of it he was fairly successful, his personal reputation had been lowered and he had jeopardised the position of Stathouder. Consequently he became more melancholy than ever and, when he contracted smallpox on 31 October 1650, he could not rouse himself from his illness. Within a week the prophecy which had always haunted him had been all but fulfilled. He was dead. Ten days later Mary gave birth to a son.

The child was born in a room draped in mourning. His mother was disconsolate at the death of her husband, but she would not relinquish her rights over the one thing she had left. Her mother-in-law tried every way she could to usurp the power which William had before his death vested in Mary. The quarrels began with the name of the child. Mary wanted to call him Charles and Amalia insisted on William. The wrangling continued even after the guests had assembled for the christening. Cold, with the sound of the rough sea-winds thudding in the background, they waited for two hours until at last the procession with the state coaches accompanied by attendants in blue Nassau liveries came into view. The Winter Queen, a godmother of the young Prince, was there with the children who were still in the Hague. Everyone was pinched with cold. Only the mother of the child did not attend. Mary, humiliated and defeated, sulked in the Binnenhof while her child was christened William Henry.

As the child grew older and fought his own battles against his physical fragility the quarrels over his upbringing never abated. His mother demonstrated a truculence in her dealings with the Dutch people which only his own personal appeal managed to redress. His grandmother was no more tactful. The French Resident at the Hague reported that she expressed herself so strongly against the State of Holland "that those who still have any regard for her are all shocked by it." Soon the States General had abolished the Stathouderate, but, instead of uniting, the Orangeist faction remained as divided as ever.

The Winter Queen entirely supported her "best niece" in all this. As the years went by the little time Mary did spend in the Hague was spent with her aunt. But the Orangeist disputes had ceased to absorb her. Instead the Stuart Princess concerned herself with her brother's problems and, when he was no longer welcome in Holland, she went with him to Paris or Brussels or wherever else he was spending the money she had managed to raise for him.

These absences left Elizabeth almost alone in the Hague. Her family, tired of her bad temper and the unruliness and impecuniosity of her household, was dispersing. Elizabeth was not altogether sorry. It had been with a definite feeling of relief that she had seen Charles Louis scuttling off to Heidelberg to reclaim his inheritance. She felt almost a repugnance for him now remembering that when amid so much hostility towards Parliament the Elector Palatine had not even condemned them, but had admitted to his mother that he had not sent condolences to Henrietta Maria for fear of offending Parliament. How different from Rupert who was risking his life to harrying Parliamentary shipping.

Charles Louis re-entered Heidelberg in October 1649. It was very different from the civilised town Elizabeth had known. "The castle," Sophia wrote later, "had suffered so severely during the Thirty Years War, that the Elector lived in the town in a house called Commissariat House."

The Elector Palatine had soon made what he considered a suitable marriage with Charlotte of Hesse-Cassel. "She was very tall," according to Sophia, "with an admirable complexion and most beautiful bust. Her features were irregular, and her eyebrows, which were dyed black, struck me as forming too violent a contrast with her beautiful flaxen hair; besides, in raising them she gave a kind of twist to her high forehead which had a very odd appearance. To make up for these defects she had beautiful sparkling eyes, full pouting lips, very fine teeth; altogether she would be called a handsome woman." Whatever her appearance the marriage proved a disaster and an embarrassment.

Sophia, who doted on her eldest brother, was the next to leave the Hague. Elizabeth let her go, petulantly asserting: "I shall never care for anybody's company that doth not care for mine. . . ." The youngest Palatine went with a yearning for adventure and, more practically, the intention of finding herself a husband. During her journey, which was paid for by Lord Craven, she was quickly disillusioned about Germany. There were no pavements, she noted disapprovingly, and the courtiers in the little courts along her route, hardly bothered about how they looked. The furniture was a disgrace and she, who had lived among the old-fashioned and decaying furniture which her mother owned, was as good a judge as any of that. She could hardly sleep at night because the beds were so uncomfortable. Her journey made her appreciate the thriftiness and the simplicity of the Dutch, and she found herself longing for the sight of a well-ordered garden. When Sophia reached Heidelberg it was to find that her brother and his new wife were continuously quarrelling. It was so bad that she mentioned it to her mother in her letters. What she did not write about however was her lurking suspicion that at times her position in Charles Louis' court resembled more that of a servant or a nursemaid than that of a sister. Quite soon Charles Louis and Charlotte were the parents of two children, Charles and Liselotte, and Sophia had been assigned to help look after them. Nevertheless she was comparatively happy, and she was soon writing to her eldest sister suggesting that she too should come to Heidelberg.

The young Elizabeth was profoundly depressed. She had never been very fortunate, but at least her very platonic relationship with Descartes had proved an absorbing diversion from other things.

She had hardly realised until now that her youth and opportunities had been neglected in the cause of misplaced filial duty. But recently her thoughts had turned more upon herself and her position.

Descartes, who had always lived a very comfortable life, rising at midday for no more strenuous occupation than thinking, walking and writing, had been induced to go to the Court of Christina of Sweden. He had arrived in time for the winter to find that he was expected to get up at five in the morning and brave the bitter cold in order to visit Christina and discuss philosophy with her. "I do not think anything would avail to keep me longer in this country than till next summer," he confided to La Grecque. However, by February he had contracted pneumonia and soon the news had been broken to the young Elizabeth that he had died. It came at almost the same time that she heard of her brother Philip's death as a mercenary fighting in France.

By then she was involved in the negotiations and preparations for her sister, Henrietta's marriage to Sigismund Rakoczy, a Prince of Transylvania. For a time she concentrated all her energies on this trying to forget her bereavements. Lace had to be ordered from Holland, because that was where it was cheapest; gold lace for the liveries had come from Frankfurt-am-Main for the same reason. Even more important the Winter Queen had somehow been persuaded to agree to the marriage, despite the fact that the bridegroom was as much a Muslim as a Protestant. But in Elizabeth's mind this disadvantage was offset by his connection with Bethlen Gabor.

The wedding took place and Henrietta and her husband were blissfully happy. Five months later, however, Henrietta, whose health since her birth had always worried her family, was dead. She left behind her a husband distraught with grief.

When La Grecque did eventually arrive in Heidelberg her brothers and her sister noticed how changed she was. "Where," asked Edward, who was paying a visit to Heidelberg, "has her liveliness gone? What has she done with her merry talk?" None of them seems to have guessed the answer.

As her children left the Hague, Elizabeth allowed her thoughts to revolve more and more around the past. Inevitably she thought of Heidelberg, but not of course Heidelberg as it was now, plundered and ravaged by the Thirty Years' War. She envisaged instead the fairy-tale castle of her honeymoon, basking in an aura of unreal calm, confident of its invulnerability, almost enchanted. That was how she saw it and it would need not one, but many letters from her children to convince her that no such place existed.

It did not taker her long to discover that coming into his inheritance had accentuated Charles Louis' churlishness. By 1 August she was writing: "I find by yours of 20th July that you are not very willing to let me have the 3,000 Rixdollars a month, which is assigned for Franckenthal." Franckenthal was her jointure and she was naturally entitled to the income which came from it. Moreover, she had never been parsmonious where Charles Louis was concerned. Everyone knew, she pointed out, "that what you have eaten since the misfortunae of your house, has been from my friends." Before he had set off for Heidelberg she had given him the Palatine furniture and jewels instead of holding them as security, as she could legally have done, until he gave her the money which was due to her from the Palatinate. "I cannot live on air," she declared as the dispute became more and more acrimonious. There was no money to pay for liveries for her servants. Even the wine, corn and cinnamon water Charles Louis was committed to sending her was delayed for so long that he lost the goodwill the giving of it might otherwise have engendered. "It may be that my next [letter]," she wrote wearily to Lord Craven, "will tell you I have no more to eat: this is no parable, but the certain truth, for there is no money nor credit of any; and this week if there be none found, I shall have neither meat nor candles. . . ." Small sums came, but never anything like enough. He sent her an occasional present as well, a picture or an inexpensive turquoise, but where more substantial help was concerned, even a plea from Charles II met with the familiar evasive phrases: "proportional to my present condition" and "considering the unsettledness of affairs in these parts". Worse still Charles Louis quibbled over what she did have. "As for the stuff, that which I have in my own chambers, you have nothing to do with," Elizabeth was soon writing heatedly, "having bought them myself." Where, Charles Louis wanted to know, was the money which was meant for Louise? He wanted more things from Rhenen. Elizabeth responded. "If I told you for whom the King your father has often said it was built and furnished, you would not believe me." What about Rupert's money, he wrote, and hangings which had been given to Edward? "An old rotten suit of hangings", Elizabeth described them as in exasperation. Furthermore, Charles Louis no longer had the excuse that his mother was not helping herself. Nearly all her jewels had been pawned or sold and she had agreed to put Rhenen up for sale, although she was pessimistic about the chances of finding a purchaser.

As for going to Germany, that became more improbable every year. As news of Charles Louis' domestic disputes continued to reach her from various sources Elizabeth determined to settle not in Heidelberg, but in her dower at Franckenthal. Charles Louis at first did not answer her letters for months, pleading a hurt arm as an excuse. Then he pretended to believe that she was coming to Heidelberg Castle. When he could dissimulate no longer, he told her: "Sure, your Majesty has forgotten in what condition the house at Franckenthal is in." A new house would have to be built there, or the old one repaired year by year as and when he could afford it. She would, of course, be welcome, he hastened to assure her, but he must warn her how dull she would find Germany. The company would be dreadful. "I believe your Majesty will have the Princess of Zollern's Marquis of Bady here very often," he wrote depressingly. "He is a very gaudy gentleman, and pretends much friendship to me."

He needn't have bothered, for the crux of the matter was that Elizabeth's debts tied her to the Hague. It was impossible for her to discharge them with the small amount she had from the States General and the paltry sums that arrived so grudgingly from Charles Louis.

By now her letters to him were becoming increasingly preoccupied with his domestic difficulties. Charlotte was obviously bad-tempered, vain, embarrassing, if not a little mad, and Charles Louis, who was no doubt partly reponsible for all these things, had taken one of her ladies-in-waiting, Louise von Degenfeld, as his mistress. Charlotte, who had known about the affair for some time, reacted at first by biting the girl's little finger to the bone and later by trying to shoot her with a pistol. Charles Louis eventually declared the marriage null and void on the grounds that his wife's conduct had been "contradictory, disobedient, obstinate, sulky, and rebellious". He then formed a morganatic alliance with Louise von Degenfeld and managed to live with her contentedly while Charlotte continued to regard herself as his legal wife. Elizabeth was outraged. "If everybody could quit their husbands and wives for their ill humours," she exclaimed, "there would be no small disorder in the world."

All this bickering between mother and son meant that by the end of the decade Elizabeth's affections had been transferred from Charled Louis to Rupert.

For the last five years he had been organising a small squadron of privateers attacking Parliamentary shipping off the Atlantic coasts of Portugal and Spain, in the Mediterranean and off West Africa. Time and again he had eluded the naval forces under Blake sent to destroy him and had sold his prizes to raise some money for the exiled King of England.

In the end the elements finished his career, during a disastrous expedition to the West Indies in which his brother Maurice joined him. Maurice's ship was lost and Maurice was never found, although occasionally there were rumours of his whereabouts. One report had it that he had been drowned; another that he was a captive in Puerto Rico; others that he was a slave in Algiers, a prisoner in Constantinople, or in the hands of the Spanish. Enquiries were made. Elizabeth asked the French ambassador to approach the Grand Turk, but no definite news ever reached her from any source. She never gave up hope of his returning and Rupert himself, although almost certain his brother must be dead, followed up every hopeful report as thoroughly as he could.

When Rupert returned at last to the Hague Elizabeth found him looking older, lacking vitality and no longer as exciting or indeed as uncontrollable as he had been. Even his health was impaired. He was disillusioned and inclined to quarrel. What more was there for him to do?

He turned his mind away from soldiering to art. He invented, in partnership with a Dutch officer, the technique of mezzotint, an idea which had been inspired by seeing a half-cleaned musket partly darkened by traces of rust and partly brightened where it had been polished. In 1658 he produced his masterpiece, "The Executioner of St John". He also became immersed in chemistry and produced a compound of copper and zinc and discovered a way of fusing black lead and reconverting it. As well as this he devised a curio popularly know as "Rupert's drops", and he made gunpowder ten times stronger than the usual type. With these innovations he tried to quell his disenchantment and to overcome the depression that partly resulted from his altercations with King Charles and Charles Louis.

Rupert's relationship with the exiled King had begun to sour after his return from the West Indies. Prizes had been disappointingly few and the French had taken a slice of what little money they raised. Disappointment in the exiled court turned to intrigue. In disgust, Rupert resigned his office of Master of the Horse and departed, although he still felt some affection for the young King.

He found it much more difficult to feel anything for Charles Louis, who refused to give him any of the money due to him under the Treaty of Westphalia. As the years went by Rupert found the Court of Vienna more congenial than his brother's contentious establishments in Heidelberg and less gloomy than the depleted household at the Wassaenor Hof.

And so out of Elizabeth's thirteen children, only six were still alive and only one, Louise, still lived with her. Elizabeth's life had become very dull. Any diversion was welcomed. A trip to see the confusion left by an explosion at Delft, or a visit to Antwerp and Brussels, as a companion to the Princess of Hohenzollern to look at the Queen of Sweden, but not to speak to her. Elizabeth had neither forgiven the slight to her daughter, nor would she forget the unpleasant remarks Christina had made about the English royal family. Nevertheless she was fascinated by a queen who had voluntarily abandoned her throne and who was not too unattractive either. "She is extravagant in her fashion and apparel," Elizabeth remarked, "but she has a good well-favoured face and a mild countenance."

Then there was a visit to Amalia de Solms' House in the Wood, for which Elizabeth had laid the foundation stone. Adorned with frescoes by Jordaens and miscellaneous allegorical figures, and furnished with strange pieces from China and the Indies, it also housed some of Gerard Honthorst's portraits of the Orange family.

On another occasion she attended the christening of one of the young relatives of the Orange family, at which there was dancing and supper. "My little nephew," Elizabeth reported to King Charles' secretary, "sat very still all the time: those States that were there were very much taken with him."

On the whole it was a very monotonous existence. Sitting in her rooms in the Wassaenor Hof, she would listen to the sleigh-bells ringing and the people shouting and laughing outside. There were no card games taking place between her children which she could watch over and criticise. Nothing really to divert her from the thieving that was going on continually under her eyes.

The scale on which the Winter Queen was robbed and neglected by her servants was alarming. The silver and gold lace were taken from her bed at Rhenen as soon as she had moved fairly permanently to the Hague and, in her words: "The hangings that were between the windows of my bedchamber he [the caretaker] has let rot that they fall to pieces." Perhaps it was the knowledge that his mother was so much abused that accounted to some extent for Charles Louis being so ungenerous.

She had certainly never been able to cope with servants. It was so much easier to ignore dishonesty. Hadn't Christina of Sweden experienced similar difficulties in her Court? Invaluable manuscripts and books had vanished and then mysteriously reappeared in possession of her servants. Occasionally, however, Elizabeth had to take some action. A woman called Grenville had to be dispatched at the dead of night "in a coach, which had order to set her down where she desired so to be". Too many insults had been uttered by this particular hanger-on to be ignored. However the whole incident caused such unpleasantness that it was not repeated.

Anyway by then Elizabeth had another more important event to think about. For years she and Louise had lived together in reasonable equanimity in the Hague. Brilliant and absent-minded, Louise had spent her time painting. Often she produced portraits of the family and possibly some of her pictures were signed by her tutor Honthorst to enable her to sell them and so partly cover her expenses. Recently her pictures had taken a more religious bias, her looks had begun to decline and with them her vivacity. She was often depressed. Most of this passed unnoticed by her mother, but it was commented on elsewhere.

The truth was that years before, when Henrietta Maria had been in the Hague, unknown to Elizabeth, Louise had gone to mass and the beauty of the service and the trappings had appealed to her so that gradually over the years she had begun to feel drawn towards the Roman Catholic religion. Recently an idea that Louise should join the Protestant convent at Herford had been mooted by her eldest sister. Louise had pleaded her mother as an excuse: someone, she argued, had to stay with her. This was not enough to deter La Grecque who began to look for suitable accommodation for Louise in Herford while the Abbess, a relation of Frederick's, and the Deaconess, actually quibbled over the number of arms and quarterings deriving from Louise's maternal ancestry. Wasn't there some question, they asked, about James I's legitimacy? If so Louise might not be eligible. It was at this point that Louise decided to declare her Catholic faith. She knew what her mother's reaction would be. She had seen how she had behaved over Edward's conversion and how horrified she had been when Henrietta Maria had tried unsuccessfully to convert the young Duke of Gloucester to Rome. Louise confided in the Princess of Hohenzollern and together they arranged for her to go to a Catholic convent in France.

She left surreptiously at a very early hour on 19 December 1657. The note she left her mother was stilted and evasive, giving no real indication as to where she had gone. The tone of it was almost cruel.

Elizabeth was frantic. She more or less accused the French Ambassador of being a party to the plot, since his box had been next to hers at the theatre and Louise could have spoken to him unobserved. When she learnt that he had had nothing to do with it, Elizabeth approached the States, who did their best, but failed to trace Louise.

In fact she was on her way via Antwerp to Paris where, eventually, she settled in the Catholic convent. There she continued to paint amid tolling bells, lighted tapers and quiet nuns, who themselves indulged in the domestic occupations of making crystalised fruits and tending to the produce in the orangery. Eventually Louise herself became the Abbess of this establishment and she lived a long, calm and untroubled life there. Wassaenor Hof was anything but untroubled. Elizabeth had persuaded the States General to avenge the wrong done by the Princess of Hohenzollern by depriving her of certain privileges. The Princess retaliated by circulating a rumour that Louise had been expecting a child. "Her own servants, chambermaster, washmaid and her footman were not satisfied till they were permitted to take their oath before a notary," Elizabeth wrote to Charles Louis, making it clear that there was no truth in the report. However she never forgave Louise and mother and daughter did not meet again.

Of her daughters, Elizabeth had always preferred Louise. La Grecque she found rather dull and Sophia was so attached to Charles Louis that she suspected her of disloyalty.

Sophia's efforts to get married and secure herself in a comfortable establishment had run a harassed course. She had rejected a proposal from the Portuguese Duke of Aveiro but, having endured for long enough the quarrels at Charles Louis' court, was inclined to accept Prince Adolph, the King of Sweden's brother, whom she disliked. The match was sanctioned by Charles Louis and King Charles, but Sophia hesitated. Prince Adolph, although ambitious enough, had behaved brutally to his previous wife. Luckily for her the plans fell through.

By then Elizabeth was writing to Charles Louis: "I pray think how you will do about Sophia, for she cannot with any honour stay with you." Nearly twenty-seven and very much conscious of the fates of her other sisters, Sophia decided to accept anyone who asked her. The person who did was George William of Hanover. "I did not reply like a heroine of a romance," she admitted, "for I at once said yes." George William was certainly pleasant, moreover he was sophisticated. Unfortunately he was dissolute as well. No sooner had he proposed and been accepted than he set off for Venice for what he intended to be his last experience of freedom. This involved embarking on an affair with a Greek woman and contracting venereal disease. It was the kind of life he enjoyed. In all honesty he could not relinquish it, and yet his subjects in Hanover were determined that he should marry. While Sophia waited impatiently for letters that never came, George William devised a plan which would absolve him of the unpleasant responsibilities and ties of matrimony. He arranged with his youngest brother, Ernest Augustus, that he should marry Sophia instead. George William would sign a document vowing never to marry and therefore ensuring that the Brunswick-Lüneburg estates including the dukedoms of Hanover, Osnabrück and Celle, would devolve on any children Sophia and Ernest Augustus might have. Two other brothers had to be pacified, but this was quickly achieved and together Ernest Augustus and George William went to Heidelberg to discuss the matter with Charles Louis. At first he demurred, but not for too long. His sister after all longed for a suitable establishment. Moreover, she professed a liking, which might grow to something more, for Ernest Augustus. The proposal at last was accepted and Sophia married in September 1658. "On my marriage-day," she reported, "I was dressed, according to German fashion, in white silver brocade, and my flowing hair was adorned with a large crown of family diamonds. My train . . . was of enormous length." At least here Charles Louis had not stinted. After the wedding the future mother of George I set off for Hanover.

Charles Louis' daughter, Liselotte, soon followed her. The atmosphere in Heidelberg was too strained for a child. When

George William and Ernest Augustus set off again for Italy, Sophia went to visit her mother in the Hague. Elizabeth, as usual, found Sophia rather tiresome but she thought Liselotte enchanting. Everything the child did was carefully recorded. "Liselotte doth already dance the saraband with the castanets as well as can be. She is apt and willing to learn anything, she is a very good child and has no squints at all." Nevertheless she did suffer from rickets and she showed off so much that the younger Elizabeth of Bohemia would have found her exasperating. As it was she indulged her. "She reads and understands French," she enthused to Charles Louis, "and I have promised her that when she speaks French you will give her a present, your sister and I have also promised her something." Sophia tried to remedy the spoiling. Liselotte's brother had a better face, she said. This provoked tears from Liselotte and words of comfort from her grandmother. "But I maintained that she had the better face," Elizabeth recalled, "which much joyed her." But did she really see this bouncing precocious child as a child at all! She treated her more as if she were one of her monkeys and she bracketed her in one letter with her favourite beagle. "I send you . . . Liselotte's picture, both my favourites together hers and Celadons, the prettiest beagle that ever was seen." Sophia stayed in the background laughing to herself at her mother's devotion to this child after being indifferent to so many of her own. She herself was pregnant now. Like her mother, she was reserved about her first pregnancy, but Elizabeth had long ago forgotten her feelings before the birth of Frederick Henry. "I believe some six months hence she will make you an uncle," Elizabeth told Chalres Louis, "but God forbid it should be believed, for her lady-ship doth not believe it." In May 1660 this pregnancy forced Sophia and Liselotte home to Hanover. In June her child, George Louis, was born. "He is as beautiful as an angel," Sophia announced dotingly.

Just as her grandson would always remain essentially Germanic, so for Elizabeth England had always been the country she saw as her own. Holland was merely a resting place, a point of embarkation.

Throughout the 1650s the squabbles among the Orange faction and the States in Holland had not interested her nearly so much as the behaviour of Cromwell and his party in England. The maritime war between the Dutch and the English at the beginning of the decade had not involved her, for Elizabeth's interests were now inalienably tied up with the fortunes of the House of Stuart and what she hoped would soon be the misfortunes of the Puritans in England. She had read with growing anticipation the news of the failure of Cromwell's ambitions, his personal sorrows and his declining health. In 1658 at the age of 59, the Lord Protector had died. With his death King Charles' hopes had risen and been dashed down by the accession of another Cromwell, Richard, the elder son of Oliver. Richard however was gentler, less energetic than his father. He was not prepared to risk anything. Within a year he had lost the Protectorship and the government of the country had fallen into disarray. Throughout England Royalist fervour was fermenting. The inscription *Exit Tyrannus, Regum Ultimus*—the tyrant is gone, the last of the kings—which had been placed on the spot outside the Royal Exchange where a statue of Charles I had once stood, was erased. In taverns Charles II's health was toasted and his picture hung in the streets.

King Charles himself was still abroad, hardly able to afford the next meal, virtually beseiged by creditors and in danger of assassination by the Spanish. One last lucky escape enabled him to reach Holland and embark for England.

Among those who saw him off was Elizabeth. She played an important part as the King's aunt, dining privately with him, sharing in the celebrations and having her hand respectfully kissed by an almost monotonous procession of English followers. The Hague was now crowded with English sightseers waiting for the King to embark. They complained about the food, commented excessively on the "neatness" of the Hague and on the whole compared it unfavourably with London. Elizabeth, who had done her best to enhance her appearance, was put down by a least one traveller as being "very debonair, but a plain lady". Age, worry and lack of money had been cruel to her.

187

On 23 May 1660, the King and his followers at last set off for England. Guns were fired, Elizabeth, her three Stuart nephews, her "best niece", and the Prince of Orange boarded the ship and dined together before the Winter Queen, supporting the sobbing Princess Mary and followed by the young Prince William, left the ship and stood watching its high masts fade into the distance.

Throughout the year people embarked for England from the Hague. Elizabeth, who every day expected an invitation from the King, became a spectator to endless comings and goings. Princess Mary went and by Christmas, like her young brother, the Duke of Gloucester, had died of smallpox. "I shall never forget her memory," Elizabeth wrote, "we lived almost twenty years together and always loved one another." Henrietta Maria and her youngest daughter Henrietta, had also gone for a short stay to England and Rupert, at King Charles' special request, had, after a fleeting visit to his mother, left for Whitehall. Elizabeth began to worry. Money promised her from England had not materialised and worse still the invitation, waited for with such anticipation, had not arrived. Her life after all now revolved around London. Gossip about her nephew James's marriage with Anne Hyde, scandal surrounding the Court, were almost her only diversions. Other things, such as the news that her eldest daughter had been admitted into a Protestant convent, hardly mattered. "As for your Sister," she told Charles Louis, "she is in a fair way of having her cousin's Abbey as being coadjutrix. I think you and I have cause to be glad to have her so settled, for then she will trouble nobody." She sent Lord Craven to London. Perhaps he could persuade the King to order the money to be paid at once and then, with her creditors settled, she could leave the Hague. Occasionally she still toyed with the idea of going to the Palatinate, but Charles Louis was so churlish generally and so lukewarm in his attitude towards King Charles, and the situation in Heidelberg was so difficult that Elizabeth envisaged a life there of continuous bickering.

The coronation, which was notable only for its frugality, came and went and Elizabeth decided she would wait no longer. An old lady, after all, could please herself. "My Lord," she wrote to the

Duke of Ormonde from her rooms with their faded furnishings surrounded by dogs, monkeys and parrots, "Now I hear that the coronation is so happily passed; I have no more patience to stay here, but am resolved to go myself to congratulate that happy action. I would not do it before, not to give the king too much trouble at once, except he had commanded me go to, and now I assure you I shall give every little trouble, for I bring with me not above twenty-six or twenty-seven persons." She would lodge in Lord Craven's house in Drury Lane and the States would provide the ships for her journey. She only planned a temporary visit. A stay of perhaps a year or two. But she still needed to reassure her creditors, whom she interviewed in her garden rather than letting them see the dilapidation of the Wassaenor Hof. Sophia and her husband and Liselotte arrived to see Elizabeth go and the French Ambassador, because Elizabeth no longer owned a coach of her own, drove her to the point of embarkation. Before she joined the ship a letter arrived from England advising her not to come just yet. The King was not ready. Angrily she brushed it aside. How could she do anything but pursue her course, having said goodbye to so many people in the Hague. She would look ridiculous if she returned.

She arrived at night, unheralded, in an England very different from the one she had left. There were still tiresome wranglings over her title, but not over precedence, since no other royal lady was residing in London at that time. There were still arguments to be pursued with Charles Louis, who was delaying the despatch of her possessions in case she might be absconding with something which he might be able to claim as his.

But her thoughts on the whole remained firmly fixed on England. She was shocked by the informalities of her nephew's Court and yet glad that his attentions to her were adequate. She was not, as she had feared, embarrassingly neglected. In the larger, scrawling handwriting which resulted from her failing eyesight, she wrote of her activities in her letters abroad. There were dinners and visits to the theatre and opera accompanied by the King.

There was time to amble along Drury Lane and to feel, despite the trimmings Edward had secured for her from France, just a little dowdy among the Restoration ladies. Then she could walk in the gardens of Drury House underneath the sycamore trees, savouring the memories of a past era conjured up by the smell of familiar English flowers. As the winter came she seldom left the house. The weather was unnaturally humid. She was soon stricken with a cold that developed into bronchitis and pneumonia. People began to wonder if the Winter Queen would see the forty-ninth anniversary of her wedding day. She died one day short of it, on 13 February 1662, having managed to extract a promise from King Charles for the repayment of her debts. She bequeathed the little she had to Lord Craven and to her children, of whom only Rupert was with her when she died. "I love you ever my dear Rupert . . ." she had written to him recently.

And so it was her soldier son who, as chief mourner, led the torch-light procession up the Thames to Henry VII's Chapel in Westminster Abbey. The service had hardly begun before the dull humidity of the last few weeks was broken by a storm that raged and squalled to such an extent that Londoners, standing in doorways for shelter from the hail, rain and lightning, commented that they could not recall such weather and wondered what it might mean.

BIBLIOGRAPHY

PRINTED SOURCES

AKRIGG, G P V	*Jacobean Pageant*
ANON	*Declaration of ban against King of Bohemia*
	A Full Declaration of the Faith and Ceremonies professed in the Dominions of Frederick V, Elector Palatine
	Good news for the King of Bohemia
	King of Bohemia's welcome to Count Mansfield
	The Life and Amours of Charles Louis
	Occurrences in the Palatinate—Copies of Letters
	Victory of King of Bohemia's Forces 1620
ARBER, E (editor)	*Stuart Tracts 1603–93*
ASHLEY, Maurice	*Charles II*
	England in the Seventeenth Century
	The Golden Century
	Life in Stuart England
ASHTON, Robert	*James I and his Contemporaries*
BAILY, F E	*Sophia of Hanover*
BAKER, L M (editor)	*Letters of Elizabeth, Queen of Bohemia*
BALD, R C	*Donne and the Drurys*
BELLER, E A (editor)	*Caricatures of the Winter King of Bohemia*
BENGER, E O	*Memoirs of Elizabeth Stuart*

BERKELEY, George-Monck	*Literary Relics*
BIRCH, Thomas	*The Life of Prince Henry*
DU BURY, the Baroness Blaze	*Memoirs of the Princess Palatine*
BONE, Quentin	*Henrietta, Queen of the Cavaliers*
BOXER, C R	*The Dutch Seaborne Empire 1600–1800*
BRETT, S R	*The Stuart Century*
BRITISH LIBRARY	*Collection of Pamphlets*
	Historical Tracts 1590–1690
	Tracts 1–71
BROMLEY, Sir George (editor)	*A Collection of Original Royal Letters*
BROOKE, Iris	*English Costume in the Seventeenth Century*
BUCHAN, Alice	*A Stuart Portrait*
BUNNETT, F E	*Louisa Juliana*
BURTON, Elizabeth	*The Elizabethans at Home*
BUTTER, Nathaniel	*Prince and Princess of the Rhine*
CAMMELL, Charles	*The Great Duke of Buckingham*
CARTE, T (editor)	*A Collection of Original Letters and Papers Concerning the Affairs of England from the Year 1641 to 1660 (Vol. 2)*
CATTY, C M (translator)	*Heidelberg Castle*
CHAPMAN, Hester	*Privileged Persons*
	The Tragedy of Charles II
CLARK, Sir George	*Seventeenth Century*
CLEUGH, James	*Prince Rupert*
COOK, Mrs.	*Royal Elizabeths*
COOPER, J P (editor)	*The New Cambridge Modern History Vol IV*
CORNWALLIS, Sir Charles	*Life of Prince Henry*
CORNWALLIS, Lady Jane	*The Private Correspondence of*
COTTON-WALKER, F M	*Cloister to Court*
COWIE, L W	*The Seventeenth Century*
ELLIS, Sir Henry (editor)	*Camden Miscellany*
	Letters Illustrative of English History
	Original Letters
ELTON, G R	*England under the Tudors*

ERLANGER, Philippe — *The Age of Courts and Kings*
ERSKINE, Lady Frances — *Memoirs relating to the Queen of Bohemia*
EVANS, R J W — *Rudolph II and his World*
FIRTH, Sir Charles — *Oliver Cromwell*
FIRTH, Sir Charles (editor) — *Stuart Tracts 1603-98*
FORESTER, H (translator) — *Memoirs of Sophia of Hanover*
FRANCHIS, D M — *Marriage between Frederick of the Palatinate and Princess Elizabeth*
FRASER, Lady Antonia (editor) — *Lives of the Kings and Queens of England*
FRIEDRICH, Carl — *The Age of the Baroque*
GEYL, Pieter — *The Netherlands in the Seventeenth Century*
GODFREY, Elizabeth — *A Sister of Prince Rupert*
GREEN, M A — *Elizabeth, Queen of Bohemia*
GREEN, V H H — *Renaissance and Reformation*
GREW, Marion — *The House of Orange*
HARBAUGH, H (translator) — *Heidelberg Catechism*
HARRISON, John — *The Departure of Frederick and Elizabeth for Prague*
HELM, P J — *History of Europe*
HILL, Christopher — *Society and Puritanism*
HINDS, Allen B (editor) — *Calendar of Venetian State Papers*
HISTORICAL MANUSCRIPTS COMMISSION — *Report on the manuscripts of Lord Montagu of Beaulieu*
HOLLINGS, J F — *The Life of Gustavus Adolphus*
HOLLINGS, Mary — *Europe in the Renaissance and Reformation*
HUIZINGA, J H — *Dutch Civilization in the Seventeenth Century*
HUXLEY, G — *Endymion Porter*
JONES, J R — *Britain and Europe in the Seventeenth Century*
KELLY, Francis, and SCHWABE, Randolph — *A Short History of Costume and Armour*

KENYON, J P — *The Stuarts*
KROLL, Maria — *Sophia, Electress of Hanover*
KRUENER, Friedrich — *J van Rusdorf*
LINKLATER, Eric — *The Royal House of Scotland*
LLOYD, David — *Memoirs of the Lives and Actions of Eminent Persons*
LONGUEVILLE, Thomas — *Policy and Paint*
LUDWIG, Emil — *The Germans*
LÜTZOW, Count — *Bohemia*
MCINNES, Ian — *Arabella*
MACLEAN, Sir Fitzroy — *A Concise History of Scotland*
MAITLAND CLUB — *Letters to King James*
MALAND, David — *Europe in the Seventeenth Century*
MATHEW, David — *James I*
MONTAGUE, R A — *The Political History of England Vol VII*
NICHOLAS, Donald — *Mr Secretary Nicholas*
OGG, David — *Europe in the Seventeenth Century*
OMAN, Carola — *Elizabeth of Bohemia*
PAGES, G — *The Thirty Years War*
PEACHAM, Henry — *Marriage of Count Palatine to Princess Elizabeth*
PHILLIPPS, Sir T (editor) — *Sir Dudley Carleton—State Letters*
PINE, L G — *Princes of Wales*
RAIT, R S — *Five Stuart Princesses*
REES, Goronwy — *The Rhine*
RICHARDSON, S (editor) — *Negotiations of Sir Thomas Roe in Turkey (Vol I)*
ROBB, Nesca — *William of Orange*
ROBERTS, Michael — *Gustavus Adolphus*
ROWSE, A L — *Ralegh and the Throckmortons*
SACKVILLE-WEST, V (editor) — *Diary of Lady Ann Clifford*
SAVAGE, Henry (editor) — *The Harleian Miscellany*
SCHILLER, J C F von — *Death of Wallenstein*
Thirty Years' War
SMITH, L Pearsall — *Sir Henry Wotton*
SOMERS, Lord (editor) — *A Collection of Rare and Valuable Tracts*

SOUTERIUS, D   *Queen of Bohemia and the death of her son*
STEEHOLM, C and H   *James I of England*
STRICKLAND, A   *Lives of the Queens of Scotland and
                                      Princesses Vol 8*
TREASURE, G R R   *Seventeenth Century France*
TREVELYAN, C M   *English Social History*
WALTON, Izaac   *Life of Donne*
WARD, Sir Adolphus William   *The Electress Sophia and the Hanoverian
                                      Succession*
                                      Sir Henry Wotton
WARNER, Rebecca   *Epistolary Curiosities* (part I)
WARRINGTON, John (editor)   *The Diary of Samuel Pepys*
WATSON, D R   *The Life and Times of Charles I*
WEDGWOOD, C V   *The King's War 1641–47*
                                      The Thirty Years' War
                                      The Trial of Charles I
WEISNER, Alois   *Guide to the royal city of Prague and to the
                                      Kingdom of Bohemia*
WEISS, John Gustav   *Die Vorgeschichte des bohmischen Aben-
                                      teurs Frederich Palatine*
WILKINSON, Clennel   *Prince Rupert the Cavalier*
WILLEY, Basil   *The Seventeenth Century Background*
WILLIAMS, Ethel   *Anne of Denmark*
WILLIAMS, R F   *Court and Times of James I (Vol II)*
WILSON, Elkin Calhoun   *Prince Henry and English Literature*
WOODWARD, Ida   *Five English Consorts of Foreign Princes*
WORDSWORTH, Christopher   *The coronation of King James and
                                      Queen Anne*
ZUMTHOR, P   *Daily Life in Rembrandt's Holland*

MANUSCRIPT SOURCES

The larger amount of my research has been done from manuscript sources, particularly the State Papers of the period. These include State Papers, Domestic; State Papers, Domestic, Scotland; State Papers, Foreign, Flanders; State Papers, Foreign, German States; State Papers, Foreign, Holland; all of which are available in the Public Record Office.

Among other manuscript sources are Additional Manuscripts; King's Manuscripts; Cotton Manuscripts; Lansdowne Manuscripts; and Stowe Manuscripts; which are in the possession of the British Library.

INDEX